Adulting Hard in Your Late Twenties and Thirties

Unlock Your Full Potential: Life Skills for Self-Discovery, Wellness, Wealth, Career Growth, and Fulfilling Relationships

Jeffrey C. Chapman

© Copyright 2023 - All rights reserved.

The content contained within this book may not be reproduced, duplicated or transmitted without direct written permission from the author or the publisher.

Under no circumstances will any blame or legal responsibility be held against the publisher, or author, for any damages, reparation, or monetary loss due to the information contained within this book, either directly or indirectly.

Legal Notice:

This book is copyright protected. It is only for personal use. You cannot amend, distribute, sell, use, quote or paraphrase any part, or the content within this book, without the consent of the author or publisher.

Disclaimer Notice:

Please note the information contained within this document is for educational and entertainment purposes only. All effort has been executed to present accurate, up to date, reliable, complete information. No warranties of any kind are declared or implied. Readers acknowledge that the author is not engaged in the rendering of legal, financial, medical or professional advice. The content within this book has been derived from various sources. Please consult a licensed professional before attempting any techniques outlined in this book.

By reading this document, the reader agrees that under no circumstances is the author responsible for any losses, direct or indirect, that are incurred as a result of the use of the information contained within this document, including, but not limited to, errors, omissions, or inaccuracies.

Contents

Dedication	IV
Introduction	1
1. The Importance of Self-awareness and Self-discovery	3
2. Finding Your Purpose and Passion	19
3. Mind, Body, and Spirit: Taking Care of Your Whole Self	31
4. Mental Health Matters: Taking Control of Your Emotional Well-being	57
5. Financial Fitness: Building Wealth for the Future	71
6. Navigating the World of Work: Career Development and Growth	89
7. Building and Maintaining Strong Relationships	105
8. Building a Strong Foundation for Family Life	115
9. Parenting and Family Life: Raising Happy and Healthy Children	123
10. Reflecting and Embracing the Next Decade with Confidence	141
Conclusion	147
Also By Jeffrey C. Chapman	148

To my dear children, Albert, Aaron, and Danielle,

This book is dedicated to you three successful and independent adults who no longer need my money, my advice, or my occasional bailouts.

But, despite your newfound independence, I wanted to thank you for your unwavering support and for always being there to provide me with your objective advice and insightful questions (even when I didn't want to hear them). Your feedback kept me on track, and your humor kept me sane (well, mostly).

So, thank you for helping me with this book. I hope it's as successful as you all are, and that it brings joy, laughter, and maybe even a little bit of wisdom to those who read it.

INTRODUCTION

A Time of Discovery, Growth, and Opportunity

If you're reading this, chances are you are in your late 20s or 30s, and you're looking for a little guidance on this wild journey we call adulthood. Let me tell you, it's a time of tremendous change and opportunity. A time when you're figuring out who you are, what you want in life, and how you're going to get it. It's a time when you're making big decisions about your career, your finances, your relationships, and your future.

You're not alone. Making these big strides is common for many of us in this stage of life. And the good news is that it's also a time when you have the most energy, passion, and potential to create the life you want.

But, let's face it, it can also be a bit overwhelming. Social media, politics, technology, and globalization have all combined to create a world that's vastly different from the one we grew up in. And that means that you're facing new challenges and opportunities that your parents and grandparents never had to deal with.

Take social justice, for example: it's a big issue for many people in their 20s and 30s. You want to make a positive impact on the world, but you're not sure how to do it.

Social media is another challenge. On the one hand, it's a great way to stay connected with friends and family, but it can also be a source of great anxiety and stress.

Technology is changing the way we work and play for the better, but it's also creating new problems, like cyberbullying and online privacy concerns.

Politics is another topic that's top of mind for many people in their late 20s and 30s. With so much division and conflict in the world, it's hard to know what to believe and whom to trust.

And then there's health and finances. You want to live a long, healthy life, but you're not sure how to take care of yourself in the best way possible. And when it comes to finances, you're not sure how to save for the future, invest your money, and pay off your debts.

But here's the thing. Despite all of these challenges, this is a great time to be alive and in your 20s or 30s. You have more freedom and opportunity than ever before to create the life you want. You have access to information, resources, and tools that your parents and grandparents never had, and you have a chance to make a real difference in the world.

In this book, we're going to explore all of these issues and more. We're going to talk about the challenges and opportunities you're facing, and I'm going to help you find your path to happiness, success, and fulfillment. I'm going to help you discover who you are, what you want, and how you're going to get there, and I'm going to do it all in a fun, engaging, and not-too-serious way because, let's be honest, life is too short to take ourselves too seriously.

So, buckle up and get ready for a wild ride! It's time to take control of your life and create the future you want. Let's go!

Chapter 1

The Importance of Self-awareness and Self-discovery

As you're coming out of your twenties with your teenage years not too far in the rearview mirror, self-awareness and self-discovery are crucial components of your personal growth and development. They allow you to understand yourself on a deeper level, identify your strengths and weaknesses, and make informed decisions about the direction you want your life to take.

As the famous psychologist Carl Jung once said, "Your vision will become clear only when you can look into your own heart. Who looks outside, dreams; who looks inside, awakes." Jung believed that self-awareness was the key to unlocking one's full potential and finding true fulfillment in life.

Similarly, renowned philosopher and psychologist William James stated, "The greatest discovery of my generation is that a human being can alter his life by altering his attitudes." By developing self-awareness, we are able to understand our thoughts, feelings, and behaviors, and we can use this insight to make positive changes in our lives.

In this chapter, I will delve into the importance of self-awareness and self-discovery, exploring topics such as:

- Understanding your values and beliefs

- Developing emotional intelligence

- Examining past experiences and their impact on your present life

- Improving communication and relationships with others

- Identifying and overcoming limiting beliefs

Through self-reflection exercises and practical tips, I aim to guide you on your journey of self-discovery, empowering you to make positive changes in your life and reach your full potential.

Understanding Your Values and Beliefs

"Know thyself" is a phrase that has been used across time and cultures because knowing yourself is still one of the most important keys to a happy, successful life. Self-awareness and self-discovery are integral parts of this process. As you move through the end of your 20s and into your 30s, it's important to think about your values and beliefs and figure out how they shape your worldview and where you fit into it.

> "Values are like fingerprints. Nobody's are the same, but you leave them all over everything you do." —Elvis Presley

Values

Your values are the principles and beliefs that are most important to you. They guide your decision-making, shape your relationships, and help you prioritize what is truly important in life. Understanding your values will allow you to make decisions that are in line with your priorities and give you a sense of fulfillment and purpose.

Beliefs

Your beliefs, on the other hand, are the attitudes and opinions you hold about the world and your place in it. They shape your perspective and influence how you interpret and react to events in your life. When you know what you believe, you'll be able to differentiate between what's helping you and what's holding you back.

> "Beliefs are choices we make about the world, about ourselves, about others, about life itself." —Peter McWilliams

How Do Our Values and Beliefs Affect Our Lives?

Our values and beliefs are a big part of what makes us who we are and where we go in life. They serve as our moral compass, guiding us toward decisions and actions that align with our sense of purpose and meaning. Understanding your values and beliefs can help you make choices that are in line with who you are and what you stand for, leading to greater satisfaction and fulfillment.

For example, if you value financial security, you may prioritize building a solid career and saving for the future, whereas if you value personal growth, you may place a higher emphasis on travel and experiences. These values can impact your career choices, relationships, and the way you spend your free time.

Another example is if you are someone who values family and community. In that case, prioritizing time with loved ones and giving back to your community may be important. On the other hand, if you value independence, you may prioritize pursuing your interests and desires, even if it means spending less time with family and friends. Understanding these values can help you make decisions about how to allocate your time and resources in a way that aligns with your priorities.

As acclaimed psychologist Abraham Maslow once said, "The ability to be in the present moment is a major component of mental wellness." By knowing what your values and beliefs are, you can have a better idea of what is important to you and what makes you happy. This can help you be more present and happy in every moment.

Figuring Out Your Values and Beliefs

Here are some exercises you can use to find out what your values and beliefs are:

1- Reflect on your past experiences:

Take some time to reflect on your past experiences, both good and bad. Think about what you learned from them and what values and beliefs were at play in those experiences. This can give you a starting point for exploring your belief system.

2- Write down your values:

Make a list of values that are important to you. It can be helpful to categorize them into areas of life, such as family, work, relationships, etc. Reflect on why each value is important to you and how it has influenced your life.

Here are some values that you can consider when doing this step:

- Honesty
- Responsibility
- Respect
- Compassion
- Empathy
- Integrity
- Trust
- Loyalty
- Gratitude
- Courage
- Perseverance
- Ambition
- Fairness
- Equality
- Kindness

- Patience

- Forgiveness

- Humility

- Generosity

- Love

Keep in mind that these values are not exhaustive, and there might be other values that are important to you. The most important thing is to choose values that align with your beliefs and principles and that you strive to live by in your daily life.

3- Identify your core beliefs:
Core beliefs are the underlying assumptions that guide our thoughts, feelings, and behaviors. Although many of our core beliefs may be positive, sometimes we might also have limiting beliefs, or beliefs that are holding us back. Write down any limiting beliefs you have and consider if they align with your values. Then, work on reframing these beliefs to be more in line with your values and goals.

Here are some limiting beliefs that you can consider when doing this exercise:

- I'm not good enough.

- I'll never be successful.

- I don't deserve love or happiness.

- I'm not smart enough.

- I'll never change.

- I can't achieve my goals.

- I'm not worthy of respect.

- I can't trust others.

- I'll always be alone.

- I'm not strong enough.
- I can't handle change.
- I'm not worthy of love.
- I'll never be financially stable.
- I can't make a difference.
- I'm not capable of love.

4- Keep a journal:
Write down your thoughts and feelings on a daily basis. This can help you identify patterns in your beliefs and values and see how they impact your life.

5- Talk to others:
Discuss your values and beliefs with others, such as family, friends, or a therapist. Getting feedback from others can give you a different perspective on your values and beliefs and help you see them in a new light.

By doing these exercises, you can gain a deeper understanding of your values and beliefs, and how they influence your life. This can be a powerful tool for personal growth and self-discovery.

Developing a High Emotional Intelligence

Emotional intelligence, or "EQ," is the ability to recognize, understand, and control your feelings. There are many benefits to having a high EQ. It helps to improve relationships, increase empathy, and foster positive communication.

According to psychologist and researcher Daniel Goleman, "Emotional intelligence is the foundation for a host of critical skills, including conflict resolution, problem-solving, and effective communication" (Goleman, 1995)[1]. Also, people with high EQ are better able to control their emotions, which means they are less stressed and have better mental health.

A study conducted by TalentSmart found that individuals with high EQ earn an average of $29,000 more per year than those with low EQ (Bradberry & Greaves, 2009)[2]. People with high EQ are also better able to handle tough conversations and challenging situations, which makes them better leaders and team players.

In short, having a high EQ can make a big difference in your personal and professional life. By understanding and controlling your emotions, you can strengthen your relationships, improve your mental and emotional health, and achieve success in all areas of your life.

What Exactly Is Emotional Intelligence?

Emotional intelligence consists of several components, such as:

1. **Self-awareness:** Understanding your emotions and how they influence your thoughts and actions.

2. **Self-regulation:** Managing your emotions and behavior, even in challenging situations.

3. **Empathy:** Understanding and sharing the feelings of others.

4. **Motivation:** Being driven to achieve your goals, even in the face of challenges.

5. **Social skills:** Being able to communicate effectively, build and maintain relationships, and navigate social situations with ease.

---

1. Goleman, D. (1995). Emotional Intelligence: Why It Can Matter More Than IQ. Bantam Books.

2. Bradberry, T., & Greaves, J. (2009). Emotional intelligence 2.0. TalentSmart.

To improve in each area, you can try the following:

1. **Self-awareness:** Regularly check in with your emotions and reflect on your behavior. Try to identify any patterns or tendencies that might be holding you back.

2. **Self-regulation:** Practice mindfulness and other stress-reduction techniques, and work on managing your reactions in challenging situations.

3. **Empathy:** Practice active listening, put yourself in others' shoes, and try to understand their perspective.

4. **Motivation:** Set clear, achievable goals and create a plan to reach them. Surround yourself with supportive people and celebrate your progress along the way.

5. **Social skills:** Work on improving your communication and relationship-building skills. Seek feedback from others and be open to learning and growing in these areas.

How to Measure Emotional Intelligence

There are several metrics you can use to measure your EQ.

Some of the most commonly used metrics include:

- **The Emotional Quotient Inventory (EQ-i 2.0):** This is a standardized self-report measure of emotional intelligence that assesses your ability to perceive, understand, and manage your emotions.

- **The Mayer-Salovey-Caruso Emotional Intelligence Test (MSCEIT):** This test measures emotional intelligence by assessing your ability to understand and manage your emotions through tasks and questions.

- **The Bar-On Emotional Quotient Inventory (EQ-i):** This is a multi-dimensional measure of emotional intelligence that assesses five key components: intrapersonal, interpersonal, stress management, adaptability, and general mood.

- **The Trait Emotional Intelligence Questionnaire (TEIQue):** This is a self-report questionnaire that measures trait emotional intelligence, which refers to your stable tendencies to perceive, understand, and regulate emotions.

These metrics can provide valuable insights into your emotional intelligence, but it's important to keep in mind that emotional intelligence is a complex and multi-dimensional construct. It is not solely defined by these metrics, and different measures may capture different aspects of emotional intelligence.

Examining Past Experiences and Their Impact on Your Present

Examining your past is an important part of the journey of self-discovery and growth. It allows you to understand how your past has shaped who you are today and what patterns you may have developed that are impacting your present and future. By reflecting on past experiences, you can gain insight into your thought processes, behaviors, and tendencies, and identify any areas that may be holding you back or causing you stress or discomfort.

One approach to examining your past experiences is to write down a list of major events or experiences in your life and reflect on how they have impacted you. Think about how each experience has shaped your beliefs, values, and emotions. Think about what you learned from each experience and how it changed the way you act and make decisions now.

Another way to reflect on your past experiences is to seek out the guidance of a therapist or coach. Talking to a professional can provide a safe and supportive space to explore and process your past, and they can offer tools and techniques to help you understand their impact on your present.

In the book "The Power of Now" by Eckhart Tolle, he writes, "The past has no power over the present moment" (Tolle, 1997)[3]. By taking the time to think about your past, you can let go of any negative feelings or limiting beliefs that may be holding you back and embrace the present with a renewed sense of clarity and purpose.

Improving Communication and Relationships with Others

Improving how you interact with other people is a key component of personal growth and getting to know yourself. Good communication skills can lead to deeper relationships, better ways to solve problems, and a broader perspective. On the other hand, poor communication can lead to misunderstandings, hurt feelings, and damaged relationships.

To improve communication and relationships with others, it is important to understand the roles of active listening, nonverbal communication, and empathy.

Active Listening

Active listening involves paying attention to what the other person is saying and responding in a meaningful way. To practice active listening, you can't talk over the speaker. Instead, you have to wait until it's your turn to talk. This shows respect for the other person and demonstrates that you value their thoughts and opinions. It's also important to ask clarifying questions to better understand what the speaker is saying. This not only helps to avoid misunderstandings but also shows that you are interested in the conversation and want to understand the other person's perspective.

Overall, active listening is a great way to improve communication, make relationships stronger, and solve problems. By practicing active listening, you can learn more about the people around you and build stronger relationships with them.

---

3. Tolle, E. (1997). The Power of Now: A Guide to Spiritual Enlightenment. Namaste Publishing.

Nonverbal Communication

Nonverbal communication, including facial expressions, body language, and tone of voice, can play a significant role in how messages are received. To improve nonverbal communication, you need to be aware of the messages your nonverbal cues send and pay attention to the nonverbal cues of others.

Here are some specific examples of nonverbal cues and what they might mean:

- **Eye Contact:** When a person maintains eye contact while speaking, it can indicate confidence, sincerity, and engagement. However, if someone avoids eye contact while speaking, it might indicate discomfort, dishonesty, or nervousness.

- **Facial Expressions:** If someone is smiling while speaking, it can indicate happiness, friendliness, or agreement. On the other hand, if someone is frowning, it might indicate sadness, disapproval, or frustration.

- **Posture:** If someone is standing tall with good posture, it can indicate confidence, power, and assertiveness. However, if someone is slouching, it might indicate boredom, disinterest, or lack of confidence.

- **Touch:** If someone pats you on the back while speaking, it might indicate encouragement, support, or comfort. On the other hand, if someone avoids physical touch, it might indicate discomfort, disinterest, or unease.

- **Tone of Voice:** If someone speaks in a slow and steady tone, it might indicate calmness, confidence, or authority. On the other hand, if someone speaks in a high-pitched or tense voice, it might indicate nervousness, stress, or anger.

- **Gestures:** If someone nods their head while speaking, it might indicate agreement or understanding. On the other hand, if someone crosses their arms while speaking, it might indicate defensiveness, discomfort, or disagreement.

Empathy

Empathy is the ability to understand and share the feelings of others. It is a key element of good communication and relationships. To develop empathy, it is essential to put yourself in others' shoes and try to see things from their perspective. This can involve asking questions, listening actively, and practicing active reflection.

> "The most basic of all human needs is the need to understand and be understood. The best way to understand people is to listen to them."
> —Ralph G. Nicholson

Studies have shown that improving communication and relationships with others can lead to increased happiness and well-being. In one study, researchers found that individuals who reported higher levels of social support had better overall health and were less likely to experience depression and anxiety than those with lower levels of social support (Cacioppo et al., 2002)[4].

> "The greatest problem in communication is the illusion that it has been accomplished." —George Bernard Shaw

Identifying and Overcoming Limiting Beliefs

One of the most important parts of personal growth and self-discovery is figuring out and getting rid of limiting beliefs. Limiting beliefs are thoughts and ideas that we hold about ourselves and the world that restrict our potential and hold us back. They are the underlying cause of many of our fears, anxieties, and negative self-talk.

Cognitive behavioral therapy, or CBT, is a type of therapy that helps to identify and change negative thought patterns and behaviors. CBT focuses on the present moment and how your thoughts and behaviors impact your emotions and overall well-being.

---

4. Cacioppo, John T et al. (2002). Loneliness and health: potential mechanisms. Psychosomatic medicine, 64(3), 407–417. Retrieved from https://doi.org/10.1097/00006842-200205000-00005.

As part of CBT, you'll learn about common types of limiting beliefs that can keep you stuck in negative patterns. Let's go over each of these types so that you have a better understanding of what they are and how to challenge them.

1. **Filtering:**
   This is when you only focus on the negative aspects of a situation and ignore the positive. For example, you might receive positive feedback at work but only remember the one negative comment someone made. To reframe this belief, try to focus on the positive aspects of the situation and acknowledge the progress you've made.

2. **Catastrophizing:**
   This is when you expect the worst outcome in a situation and blow it out of proportion. For example, if you're about to give a presentation, you might think, "I'm going to mess up, and everyone will laugh at me." To reframe this belief, try to focus on the evidence that supports a more positive outcome and acknowledge that even if things don't go as planned, it's not the end of the world.

3. **Overgeneralization:**
   This is when you make broad, sweeping statements based on a single event or experience. For example, you might think, "I always mess up in social situations." To reframe this belief, try to focus on specific experiences and look for evidence that challenges your generalization.

4. **Mind Reading:**
   This is when you assume you know what someone else is thinking without any evidence. For example, you might think, "They're not talking to me because they're mad at me." To reframe this belief, try to communicate with the person and ask for their perspective.

5. **Black and White Thinking:**
   This is when you see things as only good or bad with no gray area in between. For example, you might think, "I'm either a complete success or a total failure." To reframe this belief, try to see things as more complex and acknowledge the nuances and complexities of any situation.

6. **Personalization:**

This is when you blame yourself for events outside of your control. For example, you might think, "It's my fault that my friend is upset. I must have said something wrong." To reframe this belief, try to focus on the external factors that may have contributed to the situation and acknowledge your own limitations.

7. **Emotional Reasoning:**

This is when you believe your emotions reflect the way things truly are. For example, you might feel anxious and think, "I must be in danger." To reframe this belief, try to challenge your emotions with evidence and focus on the facts of the situation.

8. **"Should" Statements:**

These are when you have rigid expectations for yourself or others. For example, you might think, "I should always be able to handle stress without getting upset." To reframe this belief, try to adopt a more flexible and compassionate approach and recognize that it's okay to make mistakes or feel overwhelmed at times.

9. **Disqualifying the Positive:**

This is when you downplay or dismiss positive experiences or accomplishments. For example, you might receive praise for a job well done, but think, "It was just luck." To reframe this belief, try to acknowledge and celebrate your achievements and focus on the hard work and effort you put in.

10. **Magnification or Minimization:**

Magnification is when you blow things out of proportion, while minimization is when you downplay the importance of events or experiences. For example, you might think a minor mistake is a major disaster, or you might dismiss a significant accomplishment as being no big deal. To reframe this belief, try to see things in perspective and acknowledge both the positive and negative aspects of any situation.

By recognizing and reframing your limiting beliefs, you can gain a more balanced and accurate understanding of yourself and the world around you.

Visit https://adultinghardbooks.com for a free workbook that includes a Thought Record to help you deal with difficult emotions..

Chapter 2

Finding Your Purpose and Passion

Discovering your unique skills and interests can be a challenging task. There are a few things working against you, including societal and cultural pressure to meet certain expectations, internalized limiting beliefs, and a lack of self-awareness, among other things.

Pressure from society and culture can make it hard for you to follow your passions and focus on what really makes you happy. For example, you might feel like you have to choose a job based on its prestige or financial security instead of its ability to make you happy. This can result in feeling unhappy and unmotivated in the workplace.

You can also be stopped from following your true passions and interests by the limiting beliefs you have about yourself and your life. For example, you may believe that you are not talented enough to pursue your desired career or that you are too old to make a change in your life. However, these limiting beliefs can be overcome through introspection and reflection.

Self-discovery is a key part of finding your life's purpose and a rewarding job. In a study published in the Journal of Career Assessment, author John Holland found that individuals are more likely to find fulfillment in their careers when they pursue work that aligns with their values, interests, and skills. According to Holland, "Work that is congruent with an individual's skills, abilities, and values is likely to bring the greatest satisfaction and success" (Holland, 1997)[1].

Self-reflection and introspection can also help you figure out what your strengths, values, and interests are. By taking the time to reflect on these qualities, you can make informed decisions about your career and find your true calling. As the famous philosopher Aristotle once said, "Pleasure in the job puts perfection in the work."

Finding your purpose and passion requires a combination of introspection, reflection, and action. Here are several steps that can help you discover your true calling:

1. **Identify your values**

    It's important to understand what is truly important to you in life, as your values will guide you in making meaningful career and life decisions. Consider what you stand for, what is non-negotiable, and what brings you joy and fulfillment.

2. **Reflect on your past experiences**

    Think about your past experiences, both positive and negative, and how they have shaped you. What activities and experiences have brought you the most happiness and fulfillment? What do you want to continue doing in your life?

3. **Evaluate your skills and interests**

    Take stock of your natural abilities and interests. What comes easily and effortlessly to you? What do you enjoy doing in your free time? This information can provide valuable insight into what you may be passionate about and which careers may be a good fit.

4. **Seek out new experiences**

    Trying new things can help you discover new interests and passions. Whether it's taking a class, volunteering, or traveling, taking risks and stepping out of your comfort zone can lead to personal growth and a deeper understanding of what brings you joy.

5. **Get feedback from others**

---

1. Holland, J. L. (1997). Making vocational choices: A theory of vocational personalities and work environments (3rd ed.). Psychological Assessment Resources.

Seek out the opinions of those who know you well, such as friends and family, to get a different perspective on your strengths, interests, and passions.

6. **Take action**
Once you have a clear understanding of your values, skills, interests, and passions, it's time to take action. Start small by taking steps in the direction of your passions, whether it's enrolling in a class, networking, or starting a side hustle.

As the famous Chinese philosopher Confucius once said, "Find a job you love, and you will never have to work a day in your life." By taking the time to reflect on your values, skills, interests, and passions, you can find your true purpose and create a fulfilling career and life.

Some Famous People Who Followed Their Passion

Below are some examples of people who have followed their passions and made a big difference. Each of them found success by pursuing their interests, sticking with what they were good at, and listening to their hearts. In spite of challenges and obstacles in life, these individuals serve as a source of inspiration for us all to follow our passions and find our own paths.

Oprah Winfrey fell in love with TV and the media when she was young and worked as a news anchor and then a talk show host. As she said in her show, Oprah's Lifeclass, "Everybody has a calling. And your real job in life is to figure out as soon as possible what that is, who you were meant to be, and to begin to honor that in the best way possible for yourself" (Winfrey, 2011)[2].

---

2. Winfrey, O. (2011). What Oprah Knows for Sure About Finding Your Calling [Video]. Retrieved from https://www.youtube.com/watch?v=2BQRCg-gSmU&ab_channel=OWN.

Steve Jobs, the co-founder of Apple, found his passion for design and technology early in life. In a 2005 commencement speech at Stanford University, he said, "I was lucky—I found what I loved to do early in life. Woz and I started Apple in my parents' garage when I was 20. We worked hard, and in 10 years, Apple had grown from just the two of us in a garage into a $2 billion company with over 4,000 employees" (Jobs, 2005)[3].

Frida Kahlo, a famous Mexican painter, became interested in art because of her life experiences and because she liked being creative. In a 1943 letter to her friend, she wrote, "I paint myself because I am so often alone and because I am the subject I know best."

The famous movie director **Steven Spielberg** became interested in making movies at a young age. In a 2002 interview with the Academy of Achievement, he stated, "I made my first short film when I was 12 years old, and I knew from then on that I wanted to be a filmmaker."

Tyler Perry, a well-known playwright and director, became interested in telling stories because of his emotional journey in life and his love of being creative. In a 2010 interview with Oprah Winfrey, he stated, "I wrote my first play because I was so angry and frustrated, and I just needed to get it out."

Tina Fey, a well-known comedian and writer, first became interested in comedy and writing when she was young and did improv theater. In a 2008 interview with Rolling Stone, she stated, "I started doing improv in college and then went on to Second City in Chicago, and that's where I really learned the basics of sketch writing and character creation".

Taylor Swift found her passion for music and songwriting through her early introduction to playing the guitar and singing. In a 2012 interview with Rolling Stone, she stated, "I started playing guitar when I was 12 and I wrote my first song when I was 13. It was just a natural progression for me."

---

3. Jobs, S. (2005, June 12). Stanford University Commencement Address [Audio transcription]. Stanford News. Retrieved from .

Adele found her passion for playing the piano, singing, and songwriting early in life. In a 2011 interview with Rolling Stone, she stated, "I started singing when I was four, and I started writing songs when I was 14. It was just a natural progression for me."

Paul McCartney, the famous ex-Beatle, found his passion for music through his early experiences with playing the guitar and singing. In a 1964 interview with The New York Times, he stated, "I started playing guitar when I was about 14, and I just fell in love with it. It became a big part of my life."

Michael Jordan found his passion for basketball at a young age and went on to become one of the greatest basketball players of all time. In a 1992 interview with Sports Illustrated, he stated, "Basketball has been a huge part of my life ever since I picked up a ball for the first time when I was nine."

Neil Armstrong, the first man to walk on the moon, cultivated his passion for aviation and space exploration through his early experiences as a pilot. In a 1969 interview with Time magazine, he stated, "Flying has always been a passion of mine, ever since I took my first flight at the age of 16."

Serena Williams found her passion for tennis at a young age and went on to become one of the greatest tennis players of all time. In a 1999 interview with ESPN, she stated, "Tennis has been a part of my life since I was three years old and I have a great love for the game."

Bob Dylan - Singer-Songwriter, Musician. Dylan discovered his passion for music and songwriting while growing up in Minnesota, where he was inspired by the music of Woody Guthrie and Pete Seeger. He recollected, "I just wrote what I felt like writing." He went on to become one of the most famous and influential musicians of the 20th century, putting out many classic songs and albums.

Tim Burton - Film Director, Producer, Writer. According to Burton, he has always loved making movies and telling stories. Recounting his early days, he stated, "I've always felt like an outsider." When he was 13, he made his first stop-motion animation movie. He went on to become a unique and influential voice in the film industry with iconic films such as Beetlejuice and Edward Scissorhands.

Malala Yousafzai - Activist for Female Education. Yousafzai found her passion for education and activism after surviving a gunshot wound to the head by the Taliban for advocating for girls' education. As an advocate for girls' education, she believed that, "One child, one teacher, one book, one pen can change the world" (Yousafzai, 2013)[4]. She was the youngest person to win the Nobel Peace Prize, and she continues to fight for the rights of women and children around the world to get an education.

Lin-Manuel Miranda - Composer, Lyricist, Playwright. Miranda found his passion for musical theater in college, where he wrote the music and lyrics for his first musical, In the Heights. He went on to become a Tony and Grammy-winning composer and lyricist with hit musicals such as Hamilton. He's stated, "I've never wanted to do anything else."

Vincent van Gogh - Painter. Van Gogh didn't start painting until he was older after he had tried other jobs and studied art in Paris. Despite limited success and recognition during his lifetime, he later became known as one of the most famous and influential painters in history, with iconic works such as Starry Night. In a letter to his brother in 1882, van Gogh famously defined the word artist and himself as, "I am seeking, I am striving, I am in it with all my heart" (Van Gogh, Roskill 1997)[5].

Ted Turner - Entrepreneur, Media Proprietor. Turner found his passion for media and entrepreneurship while working for his father's billboard business, after which he went on to create the cable news network CNN and become a media mogul. Describing his career, he stated, "You cannot be serious about success if you're not serious about failure."

Building a Fulfilling Career and Life That Aligns with Your Purpose

---

4. Yousafzai, M. (2013, July 13). Malala Yousafzai: 16th birthday speech at the United Nations [Audio transcription]. Retrieved from .

5. Van Gogh, V., Roskill, M. (1997). The Letters of Vincent Van Gogh. Simon and Schuster.

Building a fulfilling career and life that aligns with your purpose is a journey that requires careful planning and execution. Your purpose in life is the driving force behind your passions, goals, and aspirations, and finding a career that aligns with said purpose can lead to a life filled with meaning and satisfaction.

Here are a few steps to help you build a fulfilling career and life that aligns with your purpose:

- **Assess your values**

Understanding your core values is a crucial step toward discovering your purpose. This will help you determine what truly matters to you and what kind of career and life will align with your values.

- **Explore your interests**

Take the time to reflect on what interests you, what you enjoy doing, and what you find meaningful. This could involve trying new things, exploring different careers, or taking courses to gain new skills.

- **Reflect on your strengths and weaknesses**

Understanding your strengths and weaknesses will help you identify which careers would be a good fit for you and what areas you may need to improve upon in order to achieve your goals.

- **Set goals**

Once you've figured out what you value, what you're interested in, and what your strengths and weaknesses are, you can set attainable goals that will help you build a rewarding career and life.

- **Network**

Building a strong network of individuals who share your values, interests, and goals can help you build a supportive community that will help you grow and succeed.

- **Take action**

Once you have a clear understanding of your purpose, take action to bring your goals to fruition. This could mean starting your own business, looking for work, or going to school to learn new skills.

- **Continuously reflect and adjust**

Your purpose and goals will probably change over time, so it's important to keep thinking about them and making changes to your plans to fit with your changing purpose.

Building a fulfilling career and life that aligns with your purpose takes time, effort, and dedication. However, the reward of a life filled with meaning and satisfaction is well worth the investment.

As Steve Jobs once said, "Your work is going to fill a large part of your life, and the only way to be truly satisfied is to do what you believe is great work. And the only way to do great work is to love what you do."

Setting Meaningful Goals and Creating a Vision for Your Life

Setting goals is a crucial step in building a fulfilling career and life that aligns with your purpose. There are several strategies that you can use to set effective and achievable goals. Some of the most popular goal-setting strategies include:

- **SMART Goals:**

SMART is an acronym that stands for Specific, Measurable, Achievable, Relevant, and Time-bound. SMART goals should be clear, measurable, attainable, and in line with your values.

- **OKRs (Objectives and Key Results):**

OKRs are a framework that companies and individuals use to set and track their progress toward certain goals. OKRs consist of a clear objective and a set of key results that help measure progress toward that objective.

- **Vision Boards:**

A vision board is a visual representation of your goals and aspirations. Creating a vision board can help you clarify your goals and keep them front of mind, making it easier to stay motivated and on track.

- **Habit Stacking:**

Habit stacking is a method for developing new habits by linking them to existing ones. For example, if you already have the habit of reading for 30 minutes every day, you could add the habit of setting goals for the next day to your existing habit of reading.

- **Baby Steps:**

Taking baby steps toward your goals can help you make progress and build momentum, even if your goals are large and challenging. Start with small, achievable steps and gradually build up to bigger and more challenging goals.

- **Celebrate Progress:**

Celebrating progress toward your goals can help you stay motivated and on track. Set aside time to celebrate your successes, no matter how small they may be, and reflect on the progress you've made.

- **Seek Feedback:**

Seek feedback from others who can help you stay accountable and on track. Share your goals with friends, family, or a mentor, and ask for their support and guidance as you work toward your objectives.

These are just a few of the many strategies you can use to set and achieve your goals. The most important thing is to find a strategy that works for you and to be consistent in following through with your plans. Remember, setting and achieving your goals is a lifelong journey, and it's never too late to start.

Write Your Goals Down

Writing down your goals is an important step in the goal-setting process. When you write down your goals, you make them tangible and concrete and increase your chances of actually achieving them. This is because writing down your goals helps to clarify your thoughts, prioritize your objectives, and increase your accountability to yourself.

A study conducted by Gail Matthews, a psychologist at Dominican University in California, surveyed participants from diverse industries, including education, healthcare, and business. The study found that people who wrote down their goals were 42% more likely to achieve them compared to those who didn't[6].

This study highlights the importance of writing down your goals. When you write down your goals, you make them real and give yourself a roadmap to follow as you work toward your objectives. Whether you're setting goals for your personal life or your career, taking the time to write them down can help you increase your chances of success.

Building Self-confidence and Overcoming Self-doubt

Building self-confidence and overcoming self-doubt can be a challenge for many of us, as our brains are wired to focus on the negative and avoid taking risks that might lead to failure. But with the right tools, you can overcome these obstacles and become the confident and successful individual you were meant to be!

Self-doubt often arises because of what neuroscientists call the "negativity bias." This is the idea that your brain pays more attention to negative information and experiences than it does to positive ones. This is why it's so easy to get stuck in a cycle of self-criticism and self-doubt even when you've accomplished great things.

One way to overcome the fear of failure and build self-confidence is to reframe your thoughts. Instead of focusing on the things you did wrong, try to focus on the things you did right. As the late great comedic genius, Lucille Ball once said, "I'd rather regret the things I've done than the things I haven't done."

---

6. Economy, P. (2018, Feb 28). . Inc. Retrieved from https://www.inc.com/peter-economy/this-is-way-you-need-to-write-down-your-goals-for-faster-success.html.

Another way to build self-confidence is to set achievable goals for yourself. When you accomplish a goal, no matter how small, your brain gets a dopamine boost, and you feel good about yourself. This positive feeling can help build your self-confidence and make you more likely to take on new challenges.

And finally, don't be afraid to have a sense of humor about your struggles. Laughter really is the best medicine, and it can help you put things into perspective and keep you motivated on your journey toward self-confidence. So, when it comes to overcoming self-doubt, don't take yourself too seriously, and have a laugh whenever you can!

With a little bit of reframing, goal-setting, and humor, you can overcome self-doubt and build the self-confidence you need to reach your full potential.

Navigating the Ups and Downs of Life with Resilience

While life's inevitable ups and downs can test even the most resilient individuals, success is ultimately possible for those who persevere. The ability to overcome adversity, pick yourself up after falling, and press onward in spite of setbacks is what I mean when I talk about resilience.

There are countless examples of famous people who faced all the odds against them or faced a lot of failure in their lives and still made it. Let's take a look at a few of them:

Thomas Edison is often referred to as the "Father of the Light Bulb." He faced numerous failures in his quest to invent the electric light, but he never gave up. He famously said, "I have not failed; I've just found 10,000 ways that won't work."

Oprah Winfrey faced a difficult childhood filled with abuse and poverty, but she persevered and became one of the most successful and influential women in the world. She has said, "The biggest adventure you can ever take is to live the life of your dreams."

During his lifetime, **Abraham Lincoln** dealt with many problems and setbacks. He lost eight elections before he was finally elected president. He once said, "My great concern is not whether you have failed, but whether you are content with your failure."

Walt Disney was fired from a newspaper for lack of creativity, but he didn't let that stop him. He went on to create the world-famous Disney brand and revolutionized the animation industry.

Steven Spielberg was rejected from film school multiple times, but he never gave up on his dream of becoming a filmmaker. He went on to become one of the most successful directors of all time.

Michael Jordan was cut from his high school basketball team, but he used that failure as motivation to become one of the greatest basketball players of all time. He has said, "I've missed more than 9,000 shots in my career. I've lost almost 300 games. 26 times, I've been trusted to take the game-winning shot and missed. I've failed over and over again in my life. And that is why I succeed."

Malala Yousafzai faced life-threatening danger in her fight for education and women's rights, but she never gave up. She has said, "One child, one teacher, one book, and one pen can change the world."

These examples show us that resilience and determination are key to overcoming adversity and achieving success. No matter what challenges we face, we can always find the strength to keep pushing forward and never give up on our dreams.

Chapter 3

Mind, Body, and Spirit: Taking Care of Your Whole Self

Self-care and mental health are crucial for a fulfilling life, regardless of your age. But at this point in your life, it's especially important to put them at the top of your list as you take on new responsibilities and challenges.

If you don't take care of yourself and your mental health, it can lead to burnout, lower productivity, and a lower quality of life. On the other hand, putting yourself first can improve your overall health, your relationships, your work performance, and how happy you are with your life.

It is essential to engage in regular self-care activities that nourish your mind and body. This can include eating well, working out regularly, getting enough sleep, and doing fun things in your free time that make you happy and calm you down.

In addition, it's crucial to address any mental health issues, such as stress, anxiety, or depression, by seeking support from a mental health professional or a loved one.

As the famed cognitive-behavioral therapist Albert Ellis said, "The best years of your life are the ones in which you decide your problems are your own. You do not blame them on your mother, the ecology, or the president. You realize that you control your own destiny."

1. **Exercise:**

A study that was published in Psychosomatic Medicine found that regular exercise can make depression and anxiety symptoms much better. The study looked at 156 people with major depressive disorder who were either put on a regular exercise plan or a waiting list. The results showed that the patients in the exercise group experienced significant improvements in their depression and anxiety symptoms compared to the control group (Babyak et al., 2000)[1]

2. Diet:

A review of research published in the American Journal of Psychiatry found that a diet high in whole foods and low in processed foods is good for mental health and can help prevent and treat depression and anxiety. The review looked at several studies and found that a diet full of whole foods like fruits, vegetables, and lean protein was linked to a lower risk of depression and anxiety. On the other hand, a diet high in processed foods, such as sugar and refined carbohydrates, was associated with an increased risk of mental health conditions (Jacka et al., 2010)[2]

3. Mindfulness:

A study published in Clinical Psychology Review found that mindfulness meditation can effectively reduce symptoms of anxiety and depression. The study involved a group of employees who participated in a mindfulness meditation program and were compared to a control group who did not participate in the program. The results showed that the employees who participated in the mindfulness meditation program experienced significant reductions in their anxiety and depression symptoms compared to the control group (Keng et al., 2011)

4. Self-care:

---

1. Babyak, M. et al. (2000). Exercise treatment for major depression: maintenance of therapeutic benefit at 10 months. Psychosomatic medicine, 62(5), 633–638. Retrieved from https://doi.org/10.1097/00006842-200009000-00006.

2. Jacka, F. N. et al. (2010). Association of Western and traditional diets with depression and anxiety in women. The American journal of psychiatry, 167(3), 305–311. Retrieved from https://doi.org/10.1176/appi.ajp.2009.09060881.

A study in the American Journal of Preventive Medicine found that people who do self-care activities like exercise, sleep, and relaxation on a regular basis have a better sense of well-being and are less likely to feel burned out. The study polled more than 7,000 employees and found that those who did self-care activities like exercise, sleep, and relaxation on a regular basis reported less burnout and more well-being than those who didn't do these things (de Bruin et al., 2017)[3].

Even though these studies provide useful insights, it's important to remember that they are only a small part of the research on these topics and shouldn't be taken as the final word or as a representation of everyone's experience.

Why Start Now?

Taking care of your body and mind is important at any age, but it's particularly crucial in your late 20s and 30s, as this is a time when many people are starting to establish their careers and personal lives. Here are a few statistics that highlight the importance of taking care of your body and mind at this stage of life:

1. According to the World Health Organization (WHO), the leading causes of disability worldwide are mental health conditions, such as depression and anxiety, which are often first experienced in the late 20s and 30s[4].

2. A study published in the New England Journal of Medicine found that people in their 20s and 30s who engage in healthy habits, such as regular exercise and good sleep, are less likely to experience chronic health conditions later in life (Estruch et al., 2013)[5].

---

3. de Bruin, E. I. et al. (2017). Mindful2Work: Effects of Combined Physical Exercise, Yoga, and Mindfulness Meditations for Stress Relieve in Employees. A Proof of Concept Study. Mindfulness, 8(1), 204–217. Retrieved from https://doi.org/10.1007/s12671-016-0593-x.

4. World Health Organization. (n.d.). Mental Health. Retrieved from .

5. Estruch, R. et al. (2013). Primary prevention of cardiovascular disease with a Mediterranean diet. The New England journal of medicine, 368(14), 1279–1290. Retrieved from https://doi.org/10.1056/NEJMoa1200303,

3. The National Alliance on Mental Illness (NAMI) reports that 1 in 5 adults in the U.S. experiences a mental illness in a given year and that 50% of all lifetime cases of mental illness begin by age 14 and 75% by age 24[6].

4. According to the Centers for Disease Control and Prevention (CDC), approximately 75% of adults do not meet the recommended guidelines for physical activity, which can lead to chronic health conditions such as heart disease, stroke, and diabetes[7].

These statistics highlight the importance of taking care of your body and mind at this stage of your life, as it can have a significant impact on your physical and mental well-being in the long-term. By taking care of yourself and living a healthy life, you can lower your chances of getting long-term health problems and improve your overall quality of life.

Jack, the Young Lawyer

I met a man named Jack M., who was in his early 30s and worked long hours as a corporate lawyer. He was under a lot of stress, constantly felt anxious and overwhelmed, and was struggling to keep up with the demands of his job and personal life. Despite being successful and having much to be thankful for, Jack felt unhappy and unfulfilled.

One day, a friend recommended that he try meditation and mindfulness practices as a way to manage his stress and anxiety. Jack was skeptical at first but decided to give it a try. He started by taking just 10 minutes each day to sit quietly, focus on his breathing, and clear his mind.

---

6. National Alliance on Mental Illness (NAMI). (2022 June). Mental Health by the Numbers. Retrieved from .

7. Centers for Disease Control and Prevention (CDC). (n.d.). Physical Activity. Retrieved from .

To his surprise, Jack quickly noticed a positive impact on his mental well-being. He felt more relaxed and centered and was able to manage his stress and anxiety more effectively. He also found that he was more productive and efficient at work and was able to enjoy his personal life more.

Encouraged by these results, Jack continued his mindfulness and meditation practice and eventually added other self-care activities such as exercise and healthy eating to his routine. He became a true believer in the power of self-care and mindfulness and was able to find a new level of happiness and fulfillment in life.

Sarah, the Project Manager

Meet Sarah H., a 32-year-old woman who works as a project manager in a high-tech firm. Despite being highly skilled and successful in her career, Sarah found that her job was taking a toll on her mental and physical health. She was constantly stressed, lacked energy, and struggled with insomnia.

One day, Sarah heard about the benefits of healthy eating and exercise for reducing stress and boosting energy. She decided to give it a shot and started making changes to her diet and getting more exercise every day.

At first, Sarah was skeptical about the impact that these changes would have on her stress levels, but she soon noticed that she was feeling better both physically and mentally. She had more energy, was sleeping better, and was able to manage her stress more effectively.

Sarah continued to make healthy eating and exercise a priority in her life and found that not only did it improve her mental and physical health, but it also had a positive impact on her work performance. She was more focused, productive, and creative and was able to lead her team to greater success.

Sarah's story shows how important self-care is and how it can improve overall health and happiness, even in some of the most stressful jobs. Sarah was able to deal with her stress, improve her physical and mental health, and do well at work because she made healthy choices and put herself first.

Physical Activity and Well-being

Physical well-being is an essential aspect of health and happiness, and there are two types of people when it comes to physical activity: those who are naturally active and enjoy exercising, and those who don't.

Regular exercise can help your body and mind in many ways. It can improve your heart health, make you stronger and more durable, lower your risk of long-term diseases like diabetes and heart disease, make you more flexible and balanced, and give you more energy overall. Exercise has also been shown to improve mood, lower stress and anxiety, and help people sleep better.

On the other hand, if you don't like to exercise, you may find it hard to get yourself to be physically active. However, leading a sedentary lifestyle can have serious consequences for physical and mental health. Research has shown that sitting around all day is a major cause of chronic diseases like obesity, heart disease, and type 2 diabetes. Also, being sedentary has been linked to poor mental health, more stress and anxiety, and less energy.

A study of over 100,000 individuals across 21 countries showed that prolonged sitting for 6-8 hours per day increases the risk of heart disease and premature death by 12-13%, particularly in poorer regions[8]. This shows how important it is to be physically active every day, even if you don't like it.

Another study published in the Lancet found that even low-intensity physical activity, like brisk walking, can have big benefits for physical and mental health. The study showed that just 150 minutes of moderate-intensity aerobic activity per week can reduce the risk

---

8. Mcrae, Mike. (2022, June 17). An Enormous International Study Just Confirmed the Ugly Truth About Sitting Too Much. Science Alert. Retrieved from .

of death from all causes and improve overall physical and mental health (Lee et al., 2012)[9].

Physical health is an important part of your overall health, and it's clear that regular exercise and other physical activities are good for you. Whether you naturally enjoy being active or not, making physical activity a regular part of your routine can have a positive impact on both physical and mental health. It's important to find activities that you enjoy and that fit into your lifestyle and to make a commitment to prioritizing physical activity on a regular basis.

Types of Exercise

Different types of exercise have different effects on the body and are meant to provide different benefits. Here are some of the most common types of exercise and each of their benefits:

Cardiovascular or Aerobic Exercise:

Running, cycling, swimming, and brisk walking are examples of exercises that speed up your heart rate and breathing. A great way to strengthen your heart, build endurance, burn calories, and reduce your risk of developing heart disease is through aerobic exercise.

Here are some recommendations for incorporating cardiovascular, or aerobic, exercise into your routine:

---

9. Lee, I. M. et al. (2012). Effect of physical inactivity on major non-communicable diseases worldwide: an analysis of burden of disease and life expectancy. Lancet (London, England), 380(9838), 219–229. Retrieved from https://doi.org/10.1016/S0140-6736(12)61031-9.

9. Lee, I. M. et al. (2012). Effect of physical inactivity on major non-communicable diseases worldwide: an analysis of burden of disease and life expectancy. Lancet (London, England), 380(9838), 219–229. Retrieved from https://doi.org/10.1016/S0140-6736(12)61031-9.

1. **Set realistic goals:** Start with a goal of 30 minutes of moderate aerobic activity, 5 days a week. Gradually increase the duration and intensity of your exercise over time.

2. **Mix it up:** Try different types of aerobic exercises, such as running, cycling, swimming, or dancing, to keep things interesting and challenge your muscles in different ways.

3. **Use technology:** There are many apps and wearable devices that can track your activity, monitor your heart rate, and provide feedback on your performance. Some popular apps include Strava, MapMyRun, and MyFitnessPal.

4. **Join a class:** Taking a group fitness class can be a fun way to get in your cardio and meet new people. Try a spin class, dance fitness, or boot camp to add variety to your routine.

5. **Get outdoors:** Going for a hike, a walk in the park, or a jog in the countryside can be a great way to enjoy the fresh air and improve your cardiovascular fitness.

6. **Make it social:** Invite friends or family members to join you for a workout or sign up for a charity run or walk. Having someone to exercise with can be motivating and make the experience more enjoyable.

7. **Warm up and cool down:** Always start your workout with a 5-10 minute warm-up to get your muscles ready for exercise and end with a cool-down to prevent injury and improve recovery.

8. **Listen to music:** Creating a playlist of upbeat songs can help you stay motivated and maintain a good pace during your cardio workout.

9. **Track your progress:** Keep a record of your workouts, such as the type of exercise, duration, and intensity, to track your progress over time and stay motivated.

Strength Training or Resistance Exercise:

Strength training uses weights or other forms of resistance to work the muscles and make them stronger and more toned. This type of exercise is great for building and maintaining muscle mass, increasing bone density, and reducing the risk of injury.

Here are some recommendations for incorporating strength or resistance training into your routine:

1. **Start with bodyweight exercises:** Push-ups, squats, and lunges are excellent bodyweight exercises for building strength. These exercises don't require any special equipment and can be performed anywhere.

2. **Use dumbbells or resistance bands:** Dumbbells and resistance bands are portable and versatile tools for strength training. You can use them to target specific muscle groups, such as your biceps, triceps, or quads.

3. **Join a gym:** Joining a gym can provide you with access to a wide range of weightlifting equipment as well as the support of trained fitness professionals.

4. **Try weightlifting classes:** Weightlifting classes, such as CrossFit or Olympic lifting, can be a fun and challenging way to build strength.

5. **Focus on compound movements:** Compound movements, such as deadlifts, squats, and bench presses, are exercises that work multiple muscle groups at once and can be especially effective for building overall strength.

6. **Set achievable goals:** Start with a goal of 2-3 strength training sessions per week and gradually increase the weight and number of sets and reps as you progress.

7. **Warm up and cool down:** Always start your strength training workout with a 5-10 minute warm-up to get your muscles ready for exercise and end with a cool-down to prevent injury and improve recovery.

8. **Progress gradually:** Gradually increase the weight you use and the difficulty of your exercises to avoid injury and see continuous improvement.

9. **Focus on good form:** Good form is key to avoiding injury and getting the most benefit from your strength training exercises. Consider working with a personal trainer to refine your technique.

10. **Track your progress:** Keep a record of your strength training workouts, such as the type of exercise, weight, and number of sets and reps, to see your progress over time and stay motivated.

Here are some popular and well-reviewed apps for strength training:

- **JEFIT:** A comprehensive workout tracking app that allows you to create custom workout routines and track your progress. It includes a large library of exercises with accompanying animations and instructions, making it a great option for those new to strength training.

- **StrongLifts 5x5:** A popular and beginner-friendly strength training program that focuses on five sets of five reps for each exercise. The app includes workout tracking, detailed instructions, and progress tracking.

- **MyFitnessPal:** A comprehensive health and wellness app with a strength training component. The app allows you to track your workouts, set goals, and see your progress over time.

- **Aaptiv:** An audio-based fitness app that offers a variety of strength training workouts led by certified personal trainers. The app also includes tracking and goal-setting features.

- **Nike Training Club:** A comprehensive fitness app that includes a variety of strength training workouts, along with tracking and goal-setting features. The app includes a library of exercises, along with animations and instructions, making it a great option for those new to strength training.

- **Fitbod:** A personalized workout app that creates custom strength training routines based on your fitness level and goals. The app includes tracking and goal-setting features, along with a library of exercises and animations.

Flexibility Exercise:

Flexibility exercises are designed to improve your range of motion and flexibility in your joints. These exercises include yoga, stretching, and Pilates. Flexibility exercises are important for improving your posture, lowering your risk of injury, and improving your overall physical health.

Here are some recommendations for incorporating flexibility or stretching exercises into your routine:

1. **Start with basic stretches:** Basic stretches, such as calf stretches, hamstring stretches, and neck stretches, are a great place to start improving your flexibility.

2. **Try yoga:** Yoga is a great way to improve your flexibility and balance as well as relieve stress and improve your overall well-being.

3. **Join a dance class:** Dance classes, such as ballet, contemporary, or jazz, can help you improve your flexibility and coordination.

4. **Use foam rollers:** Foam rollers can be used to massage tight muscles and improve flexibility and range of motion.

5. **Warm up and cool down:** Always start your flexibility or stretching routine with a 5-10 minute warm-up to get your muscles ready for exercise and end with a cool-down to prevent injury and improve recovery.

6. **Focus on good form:** Good form is key to avoiding injury and getting the most benefit from your flexibility exercises. Consider working with a personal trainer or professional instructor to refine your technique.

7. **Progress gradually:** Gradually increase the difficulty and duration of your stretches to avoid injury and see continuous improvement.

8. **Incorporate stretching into your daily routine:** Make stretching a regular part of your daily routine, such as before and after a workout or during breaks at work.

9. **Focus on specific areas of tightness:** Focus on areas of your body that are consistently tight, such as your hips or lower back, to see the most improvement.

10. **Track your progress:** Keep a record of your flexibility exercises, such as the

type of stretch, duration, and difficulty, to see your progress over time and stay motivated.

These are some popular and well-reviewed apps for flexibility training:

- **Yoga Studio:** A comprehensive yoga app that includes a large library of yoga classes, poses, and routines. The app includes both beginner and advanced level classes, along with animations and instructions, making it a great option for those new to yoga.

- **Down Dog:** A yoga app that creates custom yoga routines based on your level and goals. The app includes both guided and unguided classes, along with tracking and goal-setting features.

- **Pocket Yoga:** A yoga app that includes detailed animations and instructions for a variety of yoga poses and routines. The app includes both beginner and advanced level classes, along with tracking and goal-setting features.

- **Asana Rebel:** A yoga-inspired fitness app that includes a variety of flexibility workouts, along with tracking and goal-setting features. The app includes animations and instructions, along with a library of exercises and routines.

- **Stretching Exercises:** A comprehensive stretching app that includes a variety of stretching routines, along with animations and instructions. The app includes tracking and goal-setting features, along with routines for different body parts and goals.

- **Flexibility Workouts:** A comprehensive stretching and flexibility app that includes a variety of stretching routines, along with animations and instructions. The app includes tracking and goal-setting features, along with routines for different body parts and goals.

High-Intensity Interval Training (HIIT):

HIIT is a type of exercise that consists of short bursts of high-intensity activity followed by periods of rest. This type of exercise is great for improving cardiovascular health, increasing endurance, and burning calories.

Here are some recommendations for High-Intensity Interval Training (HIIT):

1. **Warm up:** Make sure to warm up for 5-10 minutes before each HIIT workout to prepare your body and reduce the risk of injury.

2. **Structure your workout:** Alternate high-intensity exercises with low-intensity recovery periods, such as 30 seconds of jumping jacks followed by 30 seconds of rest.

3. **Mix it up:** Include a variety of exercises in your HIIT workout, such as jumping jacks, squats, push-ups, and burpees, to target different muscle groups.

4. **Progress gradually:** Gradually increase the intensity and duration of your HIIT workouts over time as your fitness level improves.

And here are some popular and well-reviewed apps for HIIT:

- **Aaptiv:** A comprehensive fitness app that includes a variety of HIIT workouts, along with music and audio-based coaching.

- **Tabata Timer:** A simple app that allows you to create custom HIIT workouts using the Tabata method, which involves 20 seconds of intense exercise followed by 10 seconds of rest.

- **MyFitnessPal:** A comprehensive fitness app that includes a variety of HIIT workouts, along with tracking and goal-setting features.

- **Nike Training Club:** A comprehensive fitness app that includes a variety of HIIT workouts, along with tracking and goal-setting features.

Functional Training:

Functional training is a type of exercise that involves doing movements and exercises that are similar to things you do every day. This type of exercise is great for improving balance, coordination, and functional fitness and reducing the risk of injury in your daily life.

Here are some recommendations for functional training:

1. **Plan your workout:** Focus on exercises that mimic movements you perform in your daily life, such as squats, lunges, and deadlifts.

2. **Incorporate a variety of equipment:** Use equipment such as resistance bands, dumbbells, and kettlebells to add resistance to your functional training workout.

3. **Use compound exercises:** Compound exercises target multiple muscle groups at once to maximize the effectiveness of your workout.

4. **Incorporate into your regular routine:** Include functional training in your overall fitness routine, and aim to do functional training exercises 2-3 times per week.

There are many types of exercise to choose from, and each one has unique benefits for your physical and mental health. To get fitter all around, you need to do a variety of physical activities and find the right balance for you. Whether you prefer cardiovascular exercise, strength training, or yoga, the important thing is to stay active, challenge yourself, and have fun!

Diet and Nutrition

When it comes to diet and nutrition, there are many popular diets that people follow, each with its own set of pros and cons. Here are a few popular diets and their key characteristics:

- **Keto Diet:**

The ketogenic (or "keto") diet is a high-fat, low-carb diet that is designed to put the body into a state of ketosis, in which it burns fat for energy instead of carbohydrates. The pros of this diet include rapid weight loss and improved insulin sensitivity. The cons are that you have to stick to the diet very closely and that you might not get enough nutrients.

- **Paleo Diet:**

The paleo diet is based on the idea of eating like our ancestors did, with a focus on whole, unprocessed foods like meat, vegetables, and healthy fats. The pros of this diet are that you eat fewer processed foods and more foods that are high in nutrients. Cons include the exclusion of certain food groups and the potential for nutrient deficiencies.

- **Vegan Diet:**

A vegan diet consists of only plant-based foods and excludes all animal products. The pros of this diet include a reduced risk of certain diseases and improved heart health. Some of the cons are that you have to plan carefully to make sure you get enough nutrients and that you may have a difficult time adjusting to this diet.

- **Mediterranean Diet:**

A focus on whole foods, healthy fats, and a moderate amount of protein is what makes the Mediterranean diet what it is. The pros of this diet include improved heart health and a reduced risk of certain diseases. Cons include the potential of eating too many unhealthy fats and the need to plan carefully to make sure you get enough nutrients.

When it comes to proper nutrition, the best course of action is to focus on a balanced diet that includes a variety of nutrient-dense foods and to limit processed foods and added sugars. It is also important to listen to your body and eat in a way that makes you feel good physically and mentally. Focus on establishing healthy habits instead of following a specific diet. For example, eat a variety of nutrient-rich foods, limit added sugars and processed foods, and pay attention to your body's hunger and fullness cues.

It's also important to remember that everyone's nutritional needs are unique, and what works for one person may not work for another. It's important to talk to a medical professional to figure out what the best course of action is for you.

Nutrition Resources

If you'd like to read more about proper nutrition that will help you maintain your optimal weight and energy levels, these are some great resources:

- **The Academy of Nutrition and Dietetics:** A professional organization for registered dietitians and nutritionists that offers reliable information and resources on nutrition and healthy eating.

- **The Dietary Guidelines for Americans:** A resource published by the US Department of Agriculture and the US Department of Health and Human Services that offers science-based recommendations for healthy eating and physical activity.

- **The Centers for Disease Control and Prevention (CDC) Nutrition, Physical Activity, and Obesity page:** A comprehensive resource on healthy eating and physical activity, including tips and tools for weight management.

- **ChooseMyPlate.gov:** A website offering practical information on creating a healthy diet and making informed food choices.

- **Mayo Clinic:** A trusted source of health information, including a section on nutrition and healthy eating.

- **Nutrition.gov:** A credible resource for information on nutrition, food safety, and dietary guidelines.

- **The American Heart Association:** A non-profit organization dedicated to promoting heart health and reducing the risk of heart disease and stroke by including information on healthy eating and physical activity.

- **The Food and Nutrition Information Center:** A division of the National Agricultural Library that offers a wide range of food and nutrition information.

- **The World Health Organization:** A global authority on health that provides information on diet and nutrition.

- **Harvard T.H. Chan School of Public Health:** A leading institution for research and education in the field of public health that provides resources on nutrition and healthy eating.

Mental Well-being and Overcoming Stress and Anxiety

Mental well-being refers to the state of your mental and emotional health, which play a crucial role in your overall health and happiness.

Stress

Stress is a normal part of life that helps you react to challenges and meet deadlines. However, when stress becomes chronic, it can take a toll on both your physical and mental health. There are four main types of stress: acute, chronic, eustress, and distress. Acute stress is short-term stress that comes from a specific situation or event. Chronic stress, on the other hand, is long-term stress that stems from ongoing life challenges, such as work, family, or health issues.

Eustress, also known as positive stress, is a type of stress that can motivate and energize you. This type of stress is often associated with excitement, such as the stress felt before a big event or during a thrilling experience. Eustress can help you perform better, feel more focused, and enjoy life more.

Distress, on the other hand, is negative stress. This type of stress is often associated with chronic worry, depression, and anxiety. Distress can cause physical and mental health problems, including headaches, sleep disturbances, and a weakened immune system. Distress can also increase the risk of heart disease, high blood pressure, and stroke.

It's important to understand the difference between "eustress" and "distress," as this can help you manage stress in a healthy way. By recognizing the signs of stress and taking steps to reduce it, you can improve your physical and mental health and have a better quality of life.

Anxiety

Anxiety is a feeling of worry, nervousness, or unease about something whose outcome is unknown. Anxiety is a normal response to stress, but when it gets too bad and lasts too long, it can get in the way of daily life. There are different types of anxiety disorders, including generalized anxiety disorder, panic disorder, social anxiety disorder, and specific phobias. Anxiety can also range from mild to severe, and in some cases, it can be debilitating and interfere with a person's ability to live a normal life.

Recent studies have shed new light on the impact of stress and anxiety on the body and mind.

- One study published in the journal "Nature Reviews Neuroscience" found that chronic stress can lead to changes in the brain, particularly in the area responsible for regulating emotions, mood, and anxiety. The study showed that chronic stress can shrink the hippocampus, a region of the brain that is crucial for memory and learning, while also increasing the size of the amygdala, which is associated with fear and anxiety (de Kloet et al., 2005)[10].

- Another study published in the "International Journal of Behavioral Medicine" showed that mindfulness meditation can have a significant impact on reducing stress and anxiety levels. The study found that participants who regularly practiced mindfulness meditation experienced a significant decrease in perceived stress and anxiety, as well as improvements in their physical and psychological well-being (Hofmann et al., 2010)[11].

---

10. de Kloet, E. et al. (2005). Stress and the brain: from adaptation to disease. Nat Rev Neurosci 6, 463–475. Retrieved from https://doi.org/10.1038/nrn1683.

11. Hofmann, S. G. et al. (2010). The effect of mindfulness-based therapy on anxiety and depression: A meta-analytic review. Journal of Consulting and Clinical Psychology, 78(2), 169-183. Retrieved from https://doi.org/10.1037/a0018555.

- A third study, published in the "Journal of Clinical Psychology" found that exercise can be an effective tool for managing stress and anxiety. The study showed that individuals who regularly engaged in physical activity had lower levels of stress and anxiety compared to those who were sedentary (Weare & Nind, 2011)[12].

These studies demonstrate the importance of taking care of our mental health and the ways in which mindfulness, meditation, and physical activity can all help to reduce stress and anxiety levels.

Here are some practices that can help improve your mental well-being:

1. **Meditation and mindfulness:** Meditation and mindfulness are practices that can reduce stress and anxiety, improve focus and attention, and increase self-awareness. There are many different forms of meditation and mindfulness, including breathing exercises, guided meditations, and mindfulness-based stress reduction programs.

2. **Nutrition:** Eating a balanced diet rich in fruits, vegetables, whole grains, and lean proteins can help improve your mental well-being. On the other hand, a diet high in sugar, caffeine, and processed foods can negatively affect your mental health.

3. **Sleep:** Getting enough sleep is essential for mental well-being, as it helps your body and brain recover and recharge. Poor sleep has been linked to a variety of mental health problems, including depression, anxiety, and irritability.

4. **Social support:** Having strong social connections and a supportive network of friends and family can help improve your mental well-being and reduce feelings of loneliness and isolation.

5. **Relaxation and stress management techniques:** Relaxation and stress man-

---

12. Weare, K., & Nind, M. (2011). Health and well-being in education: An overview of key themes and concepts. International Journal of Wellbeing, 1(1), 9-24.

agement techniques, such as yoga, deep breathing exercises, and massages, can help reduce stress and improve your mental well-being.

6. **Therapy:** Therapy can help you work through mental health issues, develop coping strategies, and improve your overall mental well-being.

It's important to remember that everyone's journey to improved mental well-being is different, and what works for one person may not work for another. But if you do some or all of these things every day, you can take steps to improve your mental health and live a happier, healthier life.

Meditation and Mindfulness

Meditation and mindfulness are two practices that have gained a lot of popularity in recent years as a way to improve mental well-being.

Here are some impressive findings:

- A study published in "Neurobiology of aging" showed that, "Meditation experience is associated with differences in default mode network activity and connectivity" (Pagnoni & Cekic, 2007).[13] The study demonstrated that mindfulness meditation practice can lead to changes in the brain that are associated with improvements in attention and memory.

---

13. Pagnoni, G., & Cekic, M. (2007). Age effects on gray matter volume and attentional performance in Zen meditation. Neurobiology of aging, 28(10), 1623–1627. Retrieved from https://doi.org/10.1016/j.neurobiolaging.2007.06.008.

- A study published in "Psychiatry Research" demonstrated that, "Mindfulness practice leads to increases in regional brain gray matter density" (Hölzel, et al., 2011)[14]. The study showed that regular mindfulness meditation practice can lead to changes in the structure of the brain that are associated with improvements in emotional regulation, self-referential processing, and cognitive processing.

- A study in the "Psychoneuroendocrinology" journal examined, "The effect of mindfulness-based stress reduction on inflammatory markers in breast and prostate cancer outpatients" (Carlson, et al., 2004). The study showed that mindfulness meditation can have a positive impact on markers of inflammation in individuals with cancer, which is a key factor in the development of many chronic health conditions.

Myths and Realities

Even though there is a lot of interest in meditation and mindfulness practices, there are still a lot of myths and falsehoods associated with them. Here are a few of the most common myths and the truth behind each one:

Myth 1: Meditation requires you to completely empty your mind of all thoughts.

Reality: It's normal to have thoughts during meditation, and it's not about trying to get rid of them completely. The goal of meditation is to be able to observe your thoughts without getting caught up in them and to develop a detached and nonjudgmental point of view.

Myth 2: Mindfulness is only for people who are spiritual or religious.

Reality: Mindfulness and meditation come from different spiritual and religious practices, but they have become secularized and can be practiced by anyone, no matter what you believe or which religion you follow.

---

14. Hölzel, B. K. et al. (2011). Mindfulness practice leads to increases in regional brain gray matter density. Psychiatry research, 191(1), 36–43. Retrieved from https://doi.org/10.1016/j.pscychresns.2010.08.006.

Myth 3: Meditation and mindfulness are only for people who are struggling with mental health issues.

Reality: While meditation and mindfulness can be very helpful for people with mental health issues, these practices can also be beneficial for people without any specific mental health concerns. By fostering a sense of peace, relaxation, and increased awareness, you can improve your overall well-being and quality of life.

Now let's dive deeper into different styles of meditation and mindfulness.

Meditation Styles

Mindfulness Meditation:

A form of meditation that involves focusing on the present moment, typically through breathing or other simple physical sensations.

Loving-Kindness Meditation:

A form of meditation that involves cultivating feelings of love and kindness toward yourself and others.

Mantra Meditation:

A form of meditation that involves repeating a word or phrase to help focus your mind.

Body Scan Meditation:

A form of meditation that involves paying attention to different parts of your body, often with the goal of reducing stress and increasing relaxation.

Mindfulness Styles

Mindful Breathing:

This involves focusing on your breath and bringing awareness to the sensations of your breath moving in and out of your body.

Body Scan:

This involves lying down or sitting comfortably and focusing on different parts of your body, noticing any sensations and feelings.

Walking Meditation:

This involves walking slowly and paying attention to the sensations of your feet touching the ground, the movement of your legs, and your breath.

Yoga and Tai Chi:

Yoga and Tai Chi can also be considered forms of mindfulness, as they involve focusing on your body and breath and cultivate a sense of calm and relaxation.

By exploring different styles of meditation and mindfulness, you can find what works best for you and make these practices a regular part of your routine to support your mental well-being.

If you want to learn more about mindfulness and meditation, here are some great resources to get you started:

Books:

- "The Miracle of Mindfulness" by Thich Nhat Hanh
- "Wherever You Go, There You Are" by Jon Kabat-Zinn
- "The Power of Now: A Guide to Spiritual Enlightenment" by Eckhart Tolle
- "Mindfulness: An Eight-Week Plan for Finding Peace in a Frantic World" by Mark Williams and Danny Penman

Apps:

-

- Headspace
- Calm
- Insight Timer
- Buddhify

Online Courses:

- Coursera
- Udemy
- Skillshare
- Great Courses Plus

Workshops and Retreats:

- Local mindfulness or meditation workshops and retreats in your area
- Silent retreats, such as Vipassana, are also a great way to deepen your practice

YouTube Channels:

- Jason Stephenson
- Joe Dispenza
- The Mindful Movement
- The Honest Guys

Websites:

- Mindful.org
- Dharmaseed.org
- Samharris.org

These resources can help you get started with meditation and mindfulness and provide guidance for continuing to develop your practice over time.

CHAPTER 4

MENTAL HEALTH MATTERS: TAKING CONTROL OF YOUR EMOTIONAL WELL-BEING

Understanding the Impact of Mental Health on Your Daily Life

MENTAL HEALTH IS A critical component of your overall well-being that can impact your daily life in numerous ways. You have to work hard to keep your mental health in good shape, especially because adulthood brings more responsibilities and pressures. During this time of your life, you are starting to build your career, make deep connections with other people, and become more independent. This can lead to a lot of stress and anxiety, which, if left unaddressed, can have a significant impact on your daily life. Today's society moves quickly and is very connected, which can lead to mental health problems like depression and anxiety. We are bombarded with messages of perfection, and our worth is often tied to our successes and the standards set by society. This kind of pressure can lead to feelings of inadequacy and low self-esteem, which can negatively impact your mental health. It's important for you to be proactive in taking care of your mental health and to understand that it is okay to seek help when you need it. By addressing your mental health concerns, you can improve your quality of life and live the best life possible.

Mental Health Throughout History

Historically, mental health has often been misunderstood, and many people with mental health conditions have been treated poorly. Before the 19th century, people with mental health problems were often thought to be possessed by evil spirits or demons and were given cruel and inhumane treatments like exorcisms, imprisonment in dungeons, or physical restraints. During the 19th century, mental health treatment shifted to a more medical, although not necessarily more humane, model with the advent of asylums, where people with mental health conditions were confined and subjected to harsh treatments such as bloodletting, lobotomies, and electroconvulsive therapy (ECT). Often, these treatments were done without the patient's permission, and many of these treatments caused serious harm.

Around the middle of the 20th century, talk therapy and new psychiatric drugs started to replace physical treatments as the main methods of helping people with mental health problems. Despite these improvements, however, there was still a lot of stigma around mental health conditions, and affected people still faced a lot of discrimination and negative attitudes.

In recent decades, there have been efforts to reduce the stigma surrounding mental health and promote understanding and acceptance of mental health conditions. Mental health advocacy organizations, such as the National Alliance on Mental Illness (NAMI), have worked to educate the public about mental health and reduce discrimination against people with mental health conditions[1]. Despite these efforts, mental health stigma is still a big problem, and people with mental health conditions still face discrimination and negative attitudes in many parts of society.

Removing the Stigma of Mental Health Conditions

The stigma surrounding mental health conditions has been prevalent for centuries. However, in the past few decades, significant strides have been made in removing the stigma.

---

1. National Alliance on Mental Illness (NAMI). (2018 October). It's Not Stigma, It's Discrimination. Retrieved from .

In the past, mental health was often seen as a personal weakness or a character flaw, and people with mental health problems were often shamed, treated unfairly, and isolated. Because of this, people with mental health problems often hid their symptoms, which made the cycle of shame and stigma worse.

In recent years, there has been a growing awareness and understanding of mental health and a corresponding effort to reduce the stigma. For example, many public figures and celebrities have talked about their struggles with mental health, which has led to more people talking about and understanding the topic. Also, many advocacy groups and organizations have been working to make people more aware of mental health and teach them why it's important to treat it like a real health issue.

Despite these efforts, however, the stigma surrounding mental health conditions persists. Many people are still afraid to seek help or talk about their mental health struggles due to a fear of being judged or discriminated against. This can be especially challenging for people in their late 20s and 30s, who are often at a critical stage in their personal and professional lives and may not have the support they need to cope with the demands of daily life. Also, this generation is facing unique stresses and problems, such as financial instability, balancing work and family life, and the pressure to do well in a world that is changing quickly.

So, while there has been significant progress in reducing the stigma surrounding mental health, there is still much work to be done to ensure that everyone has access to the support and care they need to maintain their mental well-being. It's essential for you to prioritize your mental health and take steps to address any issues that may arise without fear of judgment or stigma.

Celebrities Speaking Out About Mental Health Problems

Mental health has become a more open topic in recent years, with many celebrities speaking out about their own struggles and what they have done to improve their mental well-being. Here are some notable examples:

Lady Gaga has been very open about her struggles with depression, anxiety, and PTSD. She has talked about the importance of therapy and medication, as well as the role that creativity and self-expression have played in her healing process.

Dwayne "The Rock" Johnson has talked about his struggles with depression and how he uses exercise and a positive mindset to manage his mental health. He has also talked about the importance of seeking help and reducing the stigma surrounding mental health issues.

Prince Harry has been very open about his mental health problems, such as his anxiety and panic attacks. He has talked about the importance of seeking help and encourages others to do the same.

Demi Lovato has been open about her struggles with addiction, eating disorders, and bipolar disorder. She has talked about the importance of therapy, medication, and self-care in her journey toward mental wellness.

Emma Watson, the actress, has been open about her struggle with anxiety and has spoken about how she practices self-care to manage it. In an interview from 2018, she said that mindfulness and meditation help her deal with stress and anxiety.

Ellen DeGeneres publicly came out as gay in 1997, which led to a period of intense public scrutiny. In a 2018 interview, she shared that she has struggled with anxiety and depression and that practicing mindfulness and yoga has been essential to her mental health.

Michael Phelps, the Olympic swimmer, has been open about his struggles with depression and anxiety. Phelps has said that he struggled with negative thoughts and that therapy and medication have helped him manage his mental health. In addition, he practices mindfulness through meditation, which has been a helpful tool for him.

Ryan Reynolds, the actor, has been open about his struggle with anxiety and has spoken about how he uses humor as a tool to manage it. In a 2019 interview, he said, "I've always had anxiety, I've just learned to control it better." Reynolds has also talked about how exercise and mindfulness help him keep his mental health in check.

Kate Middleton, the Duchess of Cambridge, has been open about the challenges of balancing motherhood and public life and the toll they took on her mental health. In a speech, she said, "I was really nervous about this, and I had a little bit of anxiety." She has also spoken out about how important it is to get help when you need it and has been a strong supporter of mental health programs.

Justin Timberlake has talked about his struggles with anxiety and how he has found relief through mindfulness and meditation. In an interview, he said, "Meditation has been the biggest tool for me to calm my mind and be in a more centered place."

Ryan Seacrest has talked about his struggle with anxiety and how he has found relief through therapy and medication. In an interview, he said, "I think therapy is important, and I think medication is important for some people, and I think it's important to find what works for you."

Overcoming Common Mental Health Challenges

Mental health is a broad umbrella term that covers a wide range of issues.

Common mental health challenges include:

- **Depression**: Persistent feelings of sadness and hopelessness, and a lack of interest in daily activities.

- **Anxiety**: A feeling of worry or fear that is often disproportionate to reality and can interfere with daily life.

- **Bipolar Disorder**: A condition characterized by alternating periods of mania and depression.

- **Schizophrenia**: A severe mental illness characterized by distorted thinking and perceptions, including hallucinations and delusions.

- **Eating Disorders**: Conditions that involve abnormal eating habits, such as anorexia, bulimia, and binge-eating disorder.

- **Post-Traumatic Stress Disorder (PTSD)**: A mental health condition that develops after experiencing or witnessing a traumatic event.

- **Obsessive-Compulsive Disorder (OCD)**: A condition characterized by recurring intrusive thoughts and repetitive behaviors.

To overcome these challenges, some of the most effective methods include:

1. **Therapy**: Talk therapy, such as cognitive-behavioral therapy (CBT), can help individuals identify and change negative thought patterns.

2. **Medication**: Antidepressants, anti-anxiety medications, and mood stabilizers can help regulate mood and reduce symptoms.

3. **Lifestyle changes**: Exercise, healthy eating, getting enough sleep, and reducing stress can improve overall mental health.

4. **Support groups**: Joining a support group can provide a safe and supportive environment for individuals to discuss their experiences and receive support from others who are going through similar struggles.

5. **Mindfulness practices**: Mindfulness and meditation can help individuals become more aware of their thoughts and feelings and reduce stress and anxiety.

It's important to note that everyone's experience with mental health is unique, and what works for one person may not work for another. It may take time and effort to find the right combination of treatments that work best for you. For a personalized treatment plan, it's always best to talk to a mental health professional.

Building Resilience and Maintaining Positive Mental Health

Building resilience and maintaining positive mental health are important aspects of overall well-being. Here are some practical tips for improving your mental health:

- **Prioritize self-care**: Make time for activities that you enjoy and that help you relax and recharge, such as reading, exercising, or spending time with friends and family.

- **Maintain a healthy lifestyle**: Eating a balanced diet, getting enough sleep, and avoiding excessive alcohol and substance use can all support your mental health.

- **Practice mindfulness**: Mindfulness practices such as meditation and deep breathing can help you stay present in the moment and reduce stress and anxiety.

- **Connect with others**: Building and maintaining strong social connections can provide support, reduce stress, and improve your mood.

- **Seek help when needed**: If you are struggling with a mental health challenge, reach out to a trusted friend, family member, or healthcare professional.

It's important to find what works best for you and to make mental health a priority in your life. Remember, taking care of your mental health is just as important as taking care of your physical health.

Building a Supportive Network for Self-care and Growth

Building a network of people who can help you take care of yourself and grow is an important part of keeping your mental health in good shape. A supportive network can help you deal with stress, challenges, and mental health problems by providing you with emotional, psychological, and even financial support. There are many resources available to help you build a supportive network, including:

- **Professional counseling services:** Individual or group therapy can be provided by a licensed therapist, psychologist, or psychiatrist.

- **Online support groups:** Websites like Mental Health America, Mind, and the Anxiety and Depression Association of America (ADAA) provide online communities for people to connect and support one another.

- **Peer support groups:** In-person groups, like those offered by the National Alliance on Mental Illness (NAMI), provide a safe and supportive space for individuals to share their experiences and connect with others who are facing similar challenges.

- **Social media:** Platforms like Facebook and Twitter offer a way to connect with others and form supportive relationships.

- **Community organizations:** Local mental health organizations and resources in your community, such as mental health clinics and advocacy groups, can be sources of information and support.

It's important to find resources and strategies that work for you, so take time to explore the options and find the support that you need. Remember, taking care of your mental health is just as important as taking care of your physical health, and having a supportive network can have a significant impact on your well-being.

Nutrition and Mental Health

Nutrition is an important part of mental health, and many studies have shown how certain foods can affect our mood and cognitive abilities. Here are a few examples:

- Omega-3 fatty acids: A study published in the "Journal of Clinical Psychology" found that omega-3 fatty acids found in fish oil may help reduce symptoms of depression, anxiety, and ADHD (Kim & Lee, 2014)[2].

- B vitamins: A study published in "The American Journal of Psychiatry" found that low levels of B vitamins, such as folate and B12, can lead to depression and other mood disorders (Jacka et al., 2018)[3].

- Probiotics: A study published in "Psychology Today" found that probiotics, or beneficial bacteria found in fermented foods like yogurt, can improve anxiety and depression symptoms (Sánchez-Villegas et al., 2017)[4].

- Dark chocolate: A study published in the "Journal of Affective Disorders" found that consuming dark chocolate can have a positive effect on mood and cognitive

---

2. Kim, Y.K., Lee, H.J. (2014). Dietary omega-3 fatty acid and omega-6 fatty acid intake and depressive symptoms: a population-based study. Journal of Clinical Psychology.

3. Jacka, F.N. et al. (2018). The Role of Nutrition in Mental Health. The American Journal of Psychiatry.

4. Sánchez-Villegas, A. et al. (2017) Dietary Patterns and Depression Risk: A Systematic Review of Observational Studies. Psychology Today.

5. Parker, G., et al. (2006). Mood state effects of chocolate. Journal of affective disorders, 92(2-3), 149–159. Retrieved from https://doi.org/10.1016/j.jad.2006.02.007.

function (Parker et al., 2006)[5].

- Leafy greens: A study published in "The Australian and New Zealand Journal of Psychiatry" found that consuming leafy greens, like spinach and kale, can improve mood and cognitive function (Jacka et al., 2009)[6].

These studies show that nutrition has a big effect on mental health, and it's important to eat nutrient-dense foods as part of a well-balanced diet to support overall mental wellness.

Sleep and Mental Health

Sleep plays a crucial role in maintaining good mental health and cognitive function. Lack of sleep or poor quality sleep can have a negative impact on our mood, cognitive abilities, and mental health.

A study published in the journal "Nature and Science of Sleep" found that sleep deprivation has been linked to symptoms of depression and anxiety. The study found that sleep-deprived individuals experienced a decrease in mood and an increase in anxiety symptoms compared to those who got adequate sleep (Nollet et al., 2020)[7].

Another study, published in the journal "Annals of the New York Academy of Sciences," found that sleep is very important for making emotional memories last. The study found

---

5. Parker, G., et al. (2006). Mood state effects of chocolate. Journal of affective disorders, 92(2-3), 149–159. Retrieved from https://doi.org/10.1016/j.jad.2006.02.007.

6. Jacka, F.N. et al. (2009). Association between magnesium intake and depression and anxiety in community-dwelling adults: the Hordaland Health Study. The Australian and New Zealand journal of psychiatry, 43(1), 45–52. Retrieved from .

7. Nollet, M., et al. (2020). Sleep deprivation and stress: a reciprocal relationship. Interface focus, 10(3), 20190092. Retrieved from https://doi.org/10.1098/rsfs.2019.0092.

that sleep helps to regulate emotions and improve mood by promoting the consolidation of emotional memories during sleep (Walker, 2009)[8].

A study published in "Sleep Medicine Reviews" also found that sleep is a very important part of how emotions and moods are controlled. The study found that sleep helps to regulate emotions and improve mood by reducing the impact of negative emotions and promoting the consolidation of positive emotions (Meerlo et al., 2008)[9].

As you can see, these studies demonstrate the important role that sleep plays in maintaining good mental health and cognitive function and highlight the need for you to prioritize getting adequate, high quality sleep as part of your self-care routine.

How to Maximize Those Zzz's

Improving the quality of your sleep can have a big effect on your mental health and brain function in general. Here are some ways to improve the quality of your sleep:

1. **Establish a consistent sleep schedule**: Going to bed and waking up at the same time every day can regulate your circadian rhythm and improve sleep quality.

2. **Create a sleep-conducive environment**: Keeping the bedroom cool, dark, and quiet can improve your chances of a good night's sleep.

3. **Limit your exposure to screens before bedtime**: The blue light emitted by electronic devices can disrupt the production of the sleep hormone melatonin.

4. **Avoid caffeine and alcohol before bed**: Both caffeine and alcohol can disrupt sleep and negatively impact your sleep quality.

5. **Engage in physical activity**: Regular exercise can improve your sleep quality

---

8. Walker, M. P. (2009). The role of sleep in cognition and emotion. Annals of the New York Academy of Sciences, 1156, 168–197. Retrieved from https://doi.org/10.1111/j.1749-6632.2009.04416.x.

9. Meerlo, P. et al. (2008). Restricted and disrupted sleep: effects on autonomic function, neuroendocrine stress systems and stress responsivity. Sleep medicine reviews, 12(3), 197–210. Retrieved from https://doi.org/10.1016/j.smrv.2007.07.007.

and promote relaxation.

6. **Practice relaxation techniques**: Techniques such as deep breathing, meditation, or yoga can help calm your mind and prepare your body for sleep.

7. **Limit napping**: Excessive napping during the day can disrupt your sleep-wake cycle and lead to difficulties falling asleep at night.

Adding these tips to your daily routine can help you sleep better and improve your mental health and brain function as a whole.

Social Support and Mental Health

Having a strong social support system is crucial for your mental health and well-being. In today's world, you may face many challenges with work-life balance, financial stress, and social isolation, all of which can negatively impact your mental health.

Studies have shown that social support can act as a buffer against stress and anxiety and can improve mood, self-esteem, and overall quality of life. In 2018, the "Journal of College Counseling" published the results of a study that found that social support can lessen the effects of stress and make people more resilient, which is good for their mental health (Watkins & Hill, 2018)[10].

But it can be hard to build and maintain a strong social support system, especially in today's fast-paced world where you may feel alone and disconnected. In these situations, it can be helpful to talk to mental health professionals or join a support group.

There have been several studies that have explored the relationship between socializing and happiness in different cultures. Here are a few examples:

---

10. Watkins, K., Hill, E.M. (2018). The Role of Stress in the Social Support–Mental Health Relationship. Journal of College Counseling, 21: 153-164. Retrieved from .

A study published in the "Journal of Happiness Studies" found that "strong social connections and social support were positively related to life satisfaction and happiness" in a sample of older adults from different cultures (Tveit, Foss & Naess, 2011)[11].

A study published in the "Journal of Cross-Cultural Psychology" found that "social support from friends and family was positively related to life satisfaction and happiness" in a sample of young adults from five different countries (Tsai, Knutson, Fung, 2006)[12].

A study published in the journal "Social Science & Medicine" found that "social support was positively related to both mental and physical health outcomes" in a sample of young adults from eight different countries (Kim & Schwab, 2003)[13].

These studies show that social support is an important part of being happy and healthy, no matter what culture you are from. But it's important to remember that different cultures have different types and sources of social support, so it's important to think about the culture you're a part of when figuring out how to apply these results to your life.

Therapy and Mental Health

Therapy plays an important role in promoting mental health and wellness. There are several types of therapy that have been found to be effective for addressing different mental health concerns.

---

11. Tveit, M., Foss, A., & Naess, H. (2011). Life satisfaction and happiness in old age: the role of social relationships and social support. Journal of Happiness Studies, 12(3), 393-413.

12. Tsai, J. L., Knutson, B., & Fung, H. H. (2006). Cultural variation in affect valuation. Journal of personality and social psychology, 90(2), 288–307. Retrieved from https://doi.org/10.1037/0022-3514.90.2.288.

13. Kim, Y., & Schwab, R. G. (2003). Social support, social networks, and health. Social Science & Medicine, 56(9), 1667-1678.

As mentioned before, Cognitive Behavioral Therapy (CBT) is a common type of therapy that focuses on changing negative thought patterns and behaviors. It is often used to treat depression, anxiety, and other mental health conditions.

Another popular form of therapy is Talk Therapy or Psychodynamic Therapy, which aims to uncover unconscious patterns of thought and behavior. This type of therapy is often used to address more complex mental health issues, such as trauma and personality disorders.

There are also forms of therapy that employ holistic approaches to mental health, such as Mindfulness-Based Cognitive Therapy (MBCT) and Acceptance and Commitment Therapy (ACT). These therapies aim to help you become more mindful and present in your daily life and improve your overall sense of well-being.

The stigma associated with therapy has significantly diminished in recent years, as people have become more educated about the importance of mental health. Many individuals today understand that therapy is a safe and effective way to address mental health concerns and are willing to seek help when needed.

If you're interested in exploring the different types of therapy available, here's a list of helpful resources:

1. Cognitive Behavioral Therapy (CBT): Beck Institute for Cognitive Behavior Therapy (https://beckinstitute.org/), National Association of Cognitive Behavioral Therapists (https://www.nacbt.org/).

2. Psychodynamic Therapy: International Psychoanalytic Association (https://www.ipa.world/), American Psychoanalytic Association (https://www.apsa.org/).

3. Humanistic Therapy: Association for Humanistic Psychology (https://ahpweb.org/).

4. Group Therapy: American Group Psychotherapy Association (https://www.agpa.org/).

5. Art Therapy: American Art Therapy Association (https://www.arttherapy.org/).

6. Music Therapy: American Music Therapy Association (https://www.musictherapy.org/), World Federation of Music Therapy (https://www.wfmt.info/).

It's important to note that not all types of therapy are appropriate for all individuals, and it's always best to consult a mental health professional to determine what type of therapy may be best for you.

Chapter 5

Financial Fitness: Building Wealth for the Future

You are in a unique position. Today's financial landscape is very different from what it was for previous generations at the same age.

One major difference is the cost of higher education. The average amount of student loan debt has gone up substantially, making it harder for you to pay back the money you borrowed. Additionally, the job market has shifted toward gig work and freelance opportunities, which can make it more challenging to save for retirement and build wealth in the traditional sense.

On the other hand, there are also new opportunities for wealth-building that previous generations didn't have access to. You can invest and grow your money more easily now that technology is getting better and there are more ways to do it. Recent studies show that younger generations are more likely to invest in the stock market and use robo-advisors.

According to various studies, it seems that people in your age group are fairly worried about their finances. A survey conducted by Bank of America found that around 70% of millennials are stressed about money, with 42% indicating that they worry about it daily[1]. A similar study by Northwestern Mutual found that 68% of millennials are stressed about their finances, with 77% saying that they worry about not being able to achieve their financial goals[2].

Despite this, another study by the Employee Benefit Research Institute found that only 42% of millennials are currently saving for retirement, compared to 63% of Gen Xers and 69% of baby boomers. This highlights the need for younger generations to start saving early and make retirement a priority[3].

These studies show how important it is for you to learn about money and get help with your finances especially if you are trying to pay off debt, save for the future, and build wealth.

I'll help you get through these problems and make the most of your opportunities. By learning how to create a personalized budget, invest in a diversified portfolio, and stay informed on market trends, you can set yourself up for long-term financial success.

Assessing Your Current Financial Situation and Creating a Budget

Doing a Financial Audit

---

1. Bank of America. (2018). 2018 Better Money Habits Millennial Report. Retrieved from https://bettermoneyhabits.bankofamerica.com/content/dam/bmh/pdf/2018bmhmillennialreport.pdf.

1. Bank of America. (2018). 2018 Better Money Habits Millennial Report. Retrieved from https://bettermoneyhabits.bankofamerica.com/content/dam/bmh/pdf/2018bmhmillennialreport.pdf.

2. Northwestern Mutual. (n.d.). Planning & Progress Study 2019. Retrieved from .

3. Employee Benefit Research Institute. (2019). 2019 Retirement Confidence Survey Summary Report. Retrieved from https://www.ebri.org/docs/default-source/rcs/2019-rcs/2019-rcs-short-report.pdf.

The first step in making a budget to reach your financial goals is to figure out how much money you currently have. A financial audit involves taking a comprehensive look at your income, expenses, debts, and assets to get a clear picture of your financial health.

Here's how you can do a financial audit:

1. **Gather financial documents:** This includes pay stubs, bank statements, credit card statements, bills, and any other financial documents that show your income and expenses.

2. **Organize your income:** List your sources of income, including your salary, side hustles, and any other sources of income.

3. **Track your expenses:** Write down all of your monthly expenses, including your rent/mortgage, utilities, food, transportation, entertainment, etc.

4. **Evaluate your debts:** Make a list of all of your debts, including student loans, credit card debt, car loans, and any other outstanding debts.

5. **Assess your assets:** Write down the value of any assets you have, such as savings accounts, stocks, real estate, etc.

By conducting a financial audit, you will get a clear picture of your current financial situation, which is crucial for creating a budget and achieving your financial goals.

Once you have finished your financial audit, you can make a budget by comparing your income to your expenses and debts. This will help you determine how much money you have left over each month and how you can allocate that money toward saving and investing for the future.

It's important to check in on your finances on a regular basis and make changes to your budget as needed in order to keep moving toward financial independence.

Creating Your Budget

Creating a budget is one of the most important things you can do to get control over your money and reach your financial goals. A budget helps you decide how to spend your money and makes sure that you don't spend more than you can afford.

Here's how you can create a budget and stick to it:

1. **List your income:** The first step in creating a budget is to determine how much money you have coming in each month. This includes your salary, side hustles, and any other sources of income.

2. **Track your spending:** Write down all of your monthly expenses, including rent/mortgage, utilities, food, transportation, entertainment, etc. You can use a budgeting app or spreadsheet to make this process easier.

3. **Categorize your spending:** Group your expenses into categories such as housing, transportation, food, etc. This will help you see where your money is going and identify areas where you may be able to cut back.

4. **Set spending limits:** Based on your income and expenses, determine how much you can afford to spend in each category. Set spending limits for each category and stick to them.

5. **Make adjustments:** If you find that you are overspending in a particular category, make adjustments to your budget to bring it back into balance.

6. **Monitor your progress:** Regularly review your spending and income to see if you are on track. If you need to make adjustments, do so as soon as possible.

As John Maxwell, an American author and speaker, said, "A budget is telling your money where to go instead of wondering where it went." If you make a budget and stick to it, you'll be well on your way to financial stability and independence.

Visit https://adultinghardbooks.com for a free workbook that includes forms to help you create your budget and track expenses.

Save Your Money and Save Yourself

Saving is an important part of building wealth and securing your financial future. A key element of successful saving and investing is compound interest, in which the interest on an investment is based not only on the amount invested at the beginning but also on the interest that has built up over time.

Here's a simple example to illustrate the power of compound interest:

Let's say you invest $10,000 at an annual interest rate of 5% for 10 years.

At the end of the 10 years, your investment will be worth $16,105.51. The $6,105.51 in growth is the result of compound interest.

Saving Strategies

There are several methods that can help you allocate and save your money effectively. Here are some of the most popular methods:

50-30-20 Rule:

The 50-30-20 rule states that you should allocate 50% of your income to necessities, 30% to discretionary spending, and 20% to savings. This method helps you make sure that, after covering your basic needs, you still have money to save and even some money left over for fun.

To implement the 50-30-20 rule, start by calculating your monthly income. Next, calculate 50% of your income and allocate that amount toward necessities like housing, food, transportation, and utilities. Then, calculate 30% of your income and allocate that amount toward discretionary spending like entertainment, dining out, shopping, etc. Finally, allocate the remaining 20% toward savings or investments.

60-40 Method:

The 60-40 method is similar to the 50-30-20 rule, but it allocates a higher percentage of your income to fixed expenses and necessities. Using this method, you would allocate 60% of your income to fixed expenses and 40% to discretionary spending and savings.

To implement the 60-40 method, start by calculating your monthly income. Next, calculate 60% of your income and allocate that amount toward your fixed expenses, such as housing, food, transportation, and utilities. Then, divide the remaining 40% into short-term savings, long-term savings, and discretionary spending.

Zero-Based Budgeting:

Zero-based budgeting is a method where your income and expenses are balanced so that you have a "zero" balance at the end of each month. This means that you account for all of your income and expenses and allocate every dollar to specific categories. This method helps ensure that you are not spending more than you earn and helps you save more effectively.

To use zero-based budgeting, you can start by making a list of all of your monthly income and expenses. Then, put every dollar of your income into specific categories, such as housing, food, transportation, utilities, entertainment, savings, etc. The goal is to have a "zero" balance at the end of the month, meaning that you have accounted for all of your income and expenses.

Pay Yourself First:

The "pay yourself first" method involves setting aside a portion of your income for savings before you pay any of your bills or make any purchases. This helps ensure that your savings are a priority and that you are putting some of your money to work for you.

To use this method, start by opening a savings account and set it up so that your checking account automatically sends money to it each month. For example, you can set up a direct deposit from your paycheck into your savings account. Then, allocate the rest of your income toward necessities and discretionary spending.

Envelope Budgeting:

Envelope budgeting is a way to set aside money for different types of spending by putting it into physical envelopes. Once the cash in an envelope is gone, you can't spend any more in that category for the month. This method can help you stay on track with your budget and avoid overspending.

To implement envelope budgeting, start by putting cash for specific spending categories like food, entertainment, etc. into designated envelopes. Use this cash to pay for expenses in each category, and when the cash in an envelope is gone, you know that you can't spend any more in that category for the month. Yeah#1

Regardless of which method you choose, the key is to find a method that works for you and stick with it. By allocating and saving your money on a regular basis, you can build wealth and make sure that you have money for the future.

Where Should You Invest Your Savings?

What should you do with the money you allocated for savings using any of the strategies above?

Investment planning is the process of setting financial goals and deciding how to use your assets to reach those goals. It means knowing how much risk you are willing to take, picking the right investments, and setting up a diversified portfolio.

Why is investment planning important? You might get a better return on your money if you invest it instead of putting it into a traditional savings account. This can help you reach your financial goals more quickly and build wealth over time.

Types of Investments

There are various types of investments, including stocks, bonds, mutual funds, real estate, and commodities. Each type of investment carries a different level of risk and return, so it's important to understand the pros and cons of each and choose the option that is best for you.

"Diversification is the only free lunch in investing." —Warren Buffett, legendary investor

Investment planning can be complicated and overwhelming, but with the right help and knowledge, you can make a successful plan to reach your financial goals.

High-Yield Savings Account: A high-yield savings account is a low-risk option for saving and growing your money.

Pros: Easy to access and manage, FDIC-insured.

Cons: Low interest rate, limited liquidity.

Certificates of Deposit (CDs): CDs are a low-risk investment option that pays a fixed interest rate for a set period of time.

Pros: guaranteed return, low risk.

Cons: penalty for early withdrawal, limited liquidity.

Employee Retirement Accounts (ERAs): An ERA, such as a 401(k) or an IRA, can help you save for retirement.

Pros: tax-advantaged contributions, employer-matching contributions.

Cons: penalty for early withdrawal, limited investment options.

Stocks: Investing in stocks offers the potential for higher returns but also carries a higher risk.

Pros: potential for high returns, diversification.

Cons: high risk, volatility.

Real estate: Investing in real estate offers the potential for a steady income and long-term appreciation.

Pros: potential for steady income, appreciation.

Cons: high upfront costs, management responsibilities.

In Case of Emergency...

An emergency fund is money that is set aside to cover unexpected expenses or emergencies, such as job loss, medical bills, car repairs, or other unforeseen events.

Having an emergency fund gives you financial security and peace of mind because you know that you'll have money to fall back on if something goes wrong. According to a study by Bankrate, only 39% of Americans have enough savings to cover a $1,000 unexpected expense[4]. This highlights the importance of having an emergency fund in place.

How much money should you aim to have in your emergency fund? Experts recommend having 3-6 months' worth of living expenses in an emergency fund. Calculate your monthly expenses (e.g., rent, utilities, food, transportation, etc.) and multiply that amount by 3-6 to determine how much you should save.

Building an emergency fund: To build an emergency fund, start by setting a savings goal and breaking it down into achievable steps. Automate your savings by setting up a separate account where a portion of your income is automatically transferred into it each month.

---

4. Konish, L. (2021, January 11). Just 39% of Americans could pay for a $1,000 emergency expense. CNBC. Retrieved from https://www.cnbc.com/2021/01/11/just-39percent-of-americans-could-pay-for-a-1000-emergency-expense.html.

You can also build your emergency fund by cutting costs, finding more ways to make money, or allocating any unexpected income (like tax refunds or bonuses).

Prioritizing savings for an emergency fund: It's important to prioritize saving for your emergency fund, especially if you have high-interest debt. Consider paying off your debt first and then redirecting those payments into your emergency fund.

> "An emergency fund is not a luxury; it's a necessity." —Suze Orman, personal finance expert

By acknowledging how important an emergency fund is and taking the steps to build one, you can improve your financial security and be better prepared for expenses that come up out of the blue.

How to Manage Your Debt

Reducing debt is an important part of managing your money because having a high debt burden can cause stress, make you less financially stable, and limit your ability to spend or invest in the future.

Types of Debt

There are two main types of debt: secured debt (e.g., mortgages, car loans) and unsecured debt (e.g., credit card debt, personal loans). It's important to understand the differences between these types of debt and the impact they can have on your finances.

Secured debt is when you borrow money and designate something you already own, like a house or a car, as collateral. If you don't pay back the loan, the lender can take your collateral to get their money back. Mortgages and car loans are examples of secured debt.

Unsecured debt is when you borrow money without any collateral. It's based on your credit score and income. If you don't pay back the loan, the lender can't take anything from you right away, but they can sue you to get their money back. Credit card debt and personal loans are examples of unsecured debt.

Knowing the differences between secured and unsecured debt is important because they can affect your credit score and financial health. Unsecured debt usually has higher interest rates and not paying it back can hurt your credit score and get you into legal trouble.

Assessing Your Debt

To effectively manage and reduce your debt, it's important to have a clear understanding of how much you owe and to whom. Make a list of all your debts, including how much interest you're paying and how much you have to pay each month. Make note of any debts owed to you as well. This information will help you figure out how to pay off your debt and set your priorities.

Strategies for Paying Off Debt

There are a number of ways to pay off debt, such as the snowball method, the avalanche method, and consolidation.

The snowball method involves paying off your debts in order of balance, starting with the smallest.

The avalanche method entails repaying your debts in order of interest rates, beginning with the highest.

Debt consolidation involves combining multiple debts into one loan with a low interest rate, making it easier to manage your monthly payments.

"Debt is like any other trap, easy enough to get into, but hard enough to get out of."
—Jonathon Swift

By managing your debt well and paying it down consistently, you can make your finances more stable, reduce your stress, and build wealth to spend or invest in the future.

How to Retire in Style

Retirement planning is the process of setting aside money for your future retirement needs. It's important to start planning for retirement as early as possible, as getting started early allows you to take advantage of the power of compound interest and minimize the impacts of inflation.

"Retirement planning is not about getting rich, it's about not running out of money."
—Jane Bryant Quinn, personal finance expert

To figure out what you need for retirement, think about your current expenses, your lifestyle, and any expenses you might have in the future, like medical costs. You can use online calculators or work with a financial advisor to estimate the amount of money you will need during retirement.

Types of Retirement Accounts

There are several types of retirement accounts available, including Traditional IRAs, Roth IRAs, 401(k)s, and pensions. Each type of account has different features and tax benefits, so it's important to understand the differences between them and choose the option that is best for you.

- **Traditional IRA:**

A Traditional IRA is an individual retirement account that allows you to save for retirement on a tax-deferred basis. This means that your contributions are tax-deductible in the year you make them, and any investment growth is tax-deferred until you withdraw the funds during retirement. There are contribution limits and income limits for Traditional IRAs, and you will owe taxes on the money when you withdraw it in retirement.

- **Roth IRA:**

A Roth IRA is an individual retirement account that allows you to save for retirement on a tax-free basis. This means that your contributions are made with after-tax dollars, so you don't gain tax benefits in the year you make the contribution, but any investment growth and withdrawals during retirement are tax-free. There are contribution limits and income limits for Roth IRA contributions.

- **401(k):**

A 401(k) is an employer-sponsored retirement savings plan. Employers may offer matching contributions, and there are contribution limits for 401(k) plans. The money in a 401(k) grows on a tax-deferred basis until you withdraw it during retirement, at which point you will owe taxes on the money.

- **Pension:**

A pension is a retirement plan sponsored by an employer. It provides a guaranteed income stream when you retire based on things like how long you worked at the company and how much you made. Some pensions are defined benefit plans, which provide a set benefit in retirement, while others are defined contribution plans, which allow you to make contributions and earn investment returns.

By actively planning your retirement, you can make sure you have enough money to live the way you want when you retire.

Protect Yourself with Insurance

> "The purpose of insurance is not to make you rich; it's to keep you from being poor." —Unknown

Insurance planning is the process of figuring out what risks you might face in your life and choosing insurance policies to help you deal with them. Why is insurance planning important? Having the right insurance coverage can help protect your assets and provide financial security for you and your loved ones. Without insurance, you and your family could be faced with significant financial costs if you were to become ill, injured, or pass away.

Types of Insurance

There are various types of insurance, including life insurance, health insurance, disability insurance, and property and casualty insurance. Each type of insurance is designed to provide coverage for specific types of risks, so it's important to understand the pros and cons of each and choose the options that are best for you.

- **Life Insurance:**

Life insurance protects your family financially in the event of your death. There are two main types of life insurance: permanent life insurance and term life insurance. Permanent life insurance covers you for your whole life, while term life insurance only covers you for a certain amount of time. Once you are married and have children who depend on you, you should consider getting life insurance.

- **Health Insurance:**

Health insurance provides financial protection to cover medical expenses. There are several types of health insurance, including employer-sponsored plans, individual plans, and government-sponsored plans (such as Medicare and Medicaid).

- **Disability Insurance:**

Disability insurance protects you financially if you can't work because of an illness or injury. There are two main types of disability insurance: short-term disability insurance and long-term disability insurance.

- **Property and Casualty Insurance:**

Property and casualty insurance financially protects your assets, like your home, car, and other belongings. There are several types of property and casualty insurance, including homeowners insurance, auto insurance, and renters insurance.

ADULTING HARD IN YOUR LATE TWENTIES AND THIRTIES

- **Umbrella Insurance:**

Umbrella insurance gives you more liability coverage than what your other insurance policies can cover. This can give you more protection in case you get sued or face some other legal action.

> "Insurance is not about things. It's about people and the things that happen to them." —T. Boone Pickens, oil magnate and philanthropist

Estate Planning

Estate planning is the process of making plans for how your assets will be distributed after you die. It involves making a will, naming beneficiaries, and making plans for the care of any children or other people who depend on you.

Why is estate planning important? It lets you decide how your assets will be divided and makes sure that your wishes will be carried out after you die. If you don't have a good estate plan, your assets may be given away based on state law, which may not be what you want.

It's never too early to start this process, especially if you own any assets.

> "Estate planning is like writing a love letter to your family." —Brian Koslow, estate planning attorney

Elements of Estate Planning

Estate planning usually involves making a will, naming beneficiaries, and making plans for the care of any children or other people who depend on you. It may also involve planning long-term care, setting up trusts, and giving powers of attorney.

But what do all of these terms mean?

- **Will:**

A will is a legal document that states what you want to happen to your property and any people who depend on you after you die. It usually includes naming an executor, who will be in charge of carrying out your wishes.

- **Beneficiaries:**

Beneficiaries are the individuals or organizations that will receive your assets after your death. You can name beneficiaries for specific assets, such as life insurance policies or retirement accounts, or you can name beneficiaries in your will.

- **Trusts:**

A trust is a legal arrangement that lets you manage and give away your money and property both while you are alive and after you die. There are several types of trusts, including revocable trusts and irrevocable trusts, each with its own rules and benefits.

- **Power of Attorney:**

A power of attorney is a legal document that allows you to appoint someone to manage your financial and legal affairs in the event that you become incapacitated. There are two main types of powers of attorney: durable powers of attorney and springing powers of attorney.

- **Long-term care planning:**

Long-term care planning involves making arrangements for the care of yourself or a loved one in the event that you need assistance with daily living activities. This could mean buying long-term care insurance, making a plan to qualify for Medicaid, or looking into other options to make sure you'll be taken care of.

Estate planning is an important part of overall financial planning because it helps ensure that your assets will be split up the way you want and that your loved ones will be safe if you die. A qualified estate planning attorney can help you create an estate plan that meets your individual needs and goals.

Chapter 6

Navigating the World of Work: Career Development and Growth

In this chapter, I'll talk about the current state of the American workplace and the problems that people face at work. I'll talk about how to navigate the job market and build a fulfilling career, including how to build a strong personal brand, keep your skills up-to-date, and find a good balance between work and life.

I will also delve into navigating workplace dynamics, conflicts, and stress and provide tips on staying motivated and focused in a fast-paced work environment. I will cover the importance of making informed career decisions, negotiating salaries, and understanding the value of benefits.

Lastly, I'll talk about how important it is to have hobbies and interests outside of work as well as how important it is to manage your money, build resilience, and deal with problems at work. My goal is to help you navigate the world of work and reach your career goals by giving you useful advice and direction.

What's the Current State of the Workplace?

The state of the American workplace is changing quickly, which can make it hard to grow and develop in your job. The COVID-19 pandemic has accelerated the trend toward remote work and virtual collaboration, which has changed the way many companies operate. This change has made it more important to know how to use technology and be able to adapt to new ones.

Another challenge in the workplace is the highly competitive job market, where it can be difficult to stand out and secure desired positions. Workers also have to deal with a job market that is changing quickly, with many traditional jobs going away and new ones emerging. To stay competitive in the job market, it is important to keep your skills and knowledge up to date.

Employers also want people with a wide range of soft skills, such as strong communication, problem-solving abilities, and leadership skills. Additionally, many employees find it hard to find a healthy balance between their work and personal lives.

Overall, figuring out the world of work and building a fulfilling career requires a willingness to learn, change, and take on new challenges.

Building a Fulfilling Career

Building a fulfilling career is a journey that requires self-reflection, goal-setting, and continuous learning. It's important to remember that your career is not just about earning a salary, but also about finding meaning and purpose in your work.

To build a fulfilling career, start by asking yourself some key questions: What are your passions and interests? What motivates and inspires you? What values do you hold dear? Once you have a clear understanding of what you want, you can begin to map out your career path and set achievable goals.

Next, focus on developing the skills and knowledge that are in demand in your desired field. Keep up with the latest trends in your field, go to training and development events, and look for mentors who can give you advice and guidance. It's also important to build a strong professional network, which can lead to valuable connections, opportunities, and insights.

Finally, be open to new experiences and opportunities. Don't be afraid to take calculated risks and try new things. Your career is a journey, not a destination, and it's important to be flexible and adaptable as you grow and evolve.

"Success is not final; failure is not fatal; it is the courage to continue that counts." —Winston Churchill

Remember, building a fulfilling career takes time and effort, but the rewards are immeasurable. When you enjoy what you do, all aspects of your life are elevated. So take the time to invest in yourself and your career, and you will be on your way to a lifetime of happiness and success.

Networking and Building Professional Relationships

Networking and building professional relationships are essential components of career success and development. Having a strong network of contacts and allies can provide you with new opportunities, valuable insights and advice, and help when things get tough.

But networking can sometimes feel like a scary or disingenuous thing to do, especially if you are naturally shy or introverted. The key to networking well is to go into it with a real desire to connect with people and build relationships that matter.

Networking can take place in a variety of settings, including industry events, conferences, and online communities. Using social media sites like LinkedIn is a good way to connect with people in your field and grow your network. Mentorship can also provide valuable guidance and support when navigating the job market.

When going to events or using social media, it's important to be real and honest with the people you meet. Building relationships based on mutual respect, trust, and shared interests can help foster strong and lasting connections.

It's also important to offer help and support to others in your network and look for opportunities to collaborate and share resources. After making a new connection, make sure to keep in touch with them and support the person when they need it.

You can build a strong network of contacts and allies who can help your career grow and succeed if you go into networking with a genuine desire to connect with others and build meaningful relationships.

Navigating Workplace Dynamics and Conflicts

Getting along with people and solving problems at work is a key element of building a successful and fulfilling career. Any workplace can have conflicts, but it's important to handle them in a professional and graceful way.

One of the key skills for navigating workplace conflicts is effective communication. Make sure to listen carefully and talk about your worries clearly and politely. Try to understand the other person's perspective and look for common ground. If you can't solve the problem by talking to each other directly, you might want to try mediation or bring in a manager or HR representative.

It's also important to keep a positive outlook and see conflict as a chance to grow and learn. Remember that conflicts can be a source of new ideas and creative solutions and can help to build stronger relationships with your colleagues.

Knowing how the workplace works and how to deal with office politics can help you deal with conflicts and build good relationships with your coworkers. This means being aware of power dynamics, making alliances, and maintaining professionalism.

The best strategies to deal with conflict include:

1. **Effective communication:** Listen actively, express your concerns respectfully, and seek to understand the other person's perspective.

2. **Empathy**: Put yourself in the other person's shoes and try to understand their point of view.

3. **Problem-solving:** Focus on finding solutions rather than placing blame.

4. **Active listening:** Pay attention to what the other person is saying and try to understand their perspective.

5. **Remaining calm:** Conflicts can escalate quickly, but it's important to stay calm and composed.

6. **Seeking mediation:** If the conflict cannot be resolved through direct communication, consider involving a manager or HR representative to mediate.

7. **Considering the bigger picture:** Look for common ground and try to find a solution that satisfies everyone involved.

8. **Learning from the experience:** Conflicts can be an opportunity for growth and learning, so reflect on what you can do differently in the future.

9. **Practicing assertiveness:** Speak up for yourself and express your needs clearly and respectfully.

10. **Taking a break:** If the situation becomes too heated, take a step back and come back to the conversation when all parties are calm and ready to find a solution.

Overall, it takes good communication, a positive attitude, and a willingness to look for solutions and find common ground to deal with workplace dynamics and conflicts. By approaching conflicts with empathy and a growth mindset, you can help create a more harmonious and productive work environment.

Learn About Your Personality Type

Learning about your personality type can help you in several ways:

Self-awareness:

When you know your personality type, you can learn more about your strengths, weaknesses, and tendencies. This can lead to greater self-awareness and personal growth.

Relationships:

Knowing your personality type can also help you understand how you interact with others and what kinds of relationships are most likely to be satisfying for you. By understanding your own personality and the personalities of others, you can improve communication and build stronger relationships.

Career development:

Knowing your personality type can also be helpful in choosing a career that is a good fit for you. It can provide insight into what kind of work environment, tasks, and goals are likely to be most fulfilling for you.

Stress management:

Understanding your personality type can help you identify the sources of stress in your life and develop strategies for managing them.

Overall, learning about your personality type can provide valuable insights into yourself and your relationships and can help you make more informed decisions about your life and career.

There are a number of different personality tests and frameworks that are used to learn about and classify different types of people. Here are a few of the most commonly used assessments:

- **Myers-Briggs Type Indicator (MBTI):**

Based on Carl Jung's theory of psychological types, the MBTI sorts people into one of 16 personality types based on four opposites: extraversion vs. introversion, sensing vs. intuition, thinking vs. feeling, and judging vs. perceiving. Official MBTI assessments can be taken by a qualified practitioner or online through a variety of websites, such as the MBTI official website (https://www.mbtionline.com/), which offers both individual and organizational assessments.

- **The Big Five Personality Traits:**

This model, which is also called the Five-Factor Model, evaluates five big parts of a person's personality: openness, conscientiousness, extraversion, agreeableness, and neuroticism. Many free online quizzes and tests, like the one from the University of California, Berkeley (https://greatergood.berkeley.edu/topic/personality/take_the_test), can give you a general idea of how you score on the Big Five personality traits.

- **DISC Personality Assessment:**

This test divides people into four personality types based on how they talk and act: dominant, influential, steady, and compliant. DISC assessments can be taken online through a variety of websites, such as the DISC Profile website (https://www.discprofile.com/what-is-disc/overview/).

- **Enneagram:**

This test divides people into nine different personality types, each of which has its own goals, fears, and ways of thinking and acting. Enneagram assessments can be taken online through a variety of websites, such as the Enneagram Institute (https://www.enneagraminstitute.com/), which offers a range of resources, including assessments and workshops.

It's important to keep in mind that while these assessments can provide valuable insights into your personality and behavior, they should not be used as the sole basis for making important life decisions or as a way to label or stereotype individuals. They should be used as a starting point for your own self-discovery and personal growth.

Developing Resilience and Coping Strategies for Workplace Challenges

To handle the challenges of the workplace, you need to have effective ways of dealing with stress. Resilience is the ability to deal with stress and challenges and bounce back from them. It is a key element of wellness and success in the workplace.

There are a number of things people can do to build resilience and deal with stress and problems at work, such as:

1. **Mindfulness and relaxation techniques:** Practice mindfulness, deep breathing, and meditation to reduce stress and improve overall well-being.

2. **Exercise and physical activity:** Regular exercise can reduce stress and improve physical and mental health.

3. **Time management and prioritization:** Make sure to prioritize tasks and manage your time effectively to reduce stress and increase productivity.

4. **Building a support network:** Surround yourself with a supportive network of friends, family, and colleagues who can provide encouragement and support during difficult times.

5. **Positive self-talk:** Reframe negative thoughts and adopt a positive mindset to improve resilience and coping abilities.

6. **Seeking help:** Don't be afraid to seek out professional help, such as counseling or therapy, if you are struggling with stress or other mental health concerns.

7. **Taking breaks and practicing self-care:** Make time for yourself and engage in activities that bring you joy and relaxation, such as reading, spending time with loved ones, or pursuing hobbies.

Staying Motivated and Focused in a Fast-paced Work Environment

Staying motivated and focused in a fast-paced work environment can be challenging, but it is crucial for success and well-being. One key strategy for staying motivated is to have a clear understanding of your goals and purpose. Having a clear sense of what you want to achieve can provide direction and focus and help you stay motivated even when faced with obstacles or challenges.

It's also important to cultivate a positive attitude and approach to work. Adopting a growth mindset, in which you view challenges as opportunities for growth and learning, can help increase motivation and resilience.

Taking care of your physical and emotional health is also important if you want to stay motivated and focused at work. This includes getting regular exercise, doing other physical activities, learning how to deal with stress, and taking breaks when you need to.

To stay motivated and on task, creating a supportive and positive work environment is key. Having positive and helpful coworkers around you, getting feedback and guidance from a mentor, and building strong relationships with coworkers can all boost motivation and well-being.

Overall, staying motivated and focused in a fast-paced work environment requires a combination of self-care, goal-setting, and a positive attitude. By taking proactive steps to prioritize your well-being and cultivate a supportive work environment, you can increase your motivation, focus, and overall success in the workplace.

Creating a Healthy Work-Life Balance

Creating a healthy work-life balance is crucial for overall well-being and success in both your personal and professional life. In today's fast-paced, technology-driven world, though, it can be hard to maintain a good balance between work and other responsibilities.

One of the key strategies for creating a healthy work-life balance is to set clear boundaries between work and personal time. This could mean setting specific work hours, turning off work-related technology when not working, and putting self-care and leisure activities at the top of your priorities.

It's also important to cultivate a positive work environment that supports work-life balance. This could mean advocating for a flexible work arrangement like working from home or having a flexible schedule, or looking for organizations that put the health and happiness of their employees first.

Taking care of your physical and mental health is also important if you want to avoid burnout and maintain a healthy work-life balance. This includes getting regular exercise and being active, learning how to deal with stress, and taking breaks when you need to.

Studies have shown that work-life balance and burnout are closely related. For example, a study in the "Journal of Applied Psychology" found that people who said they had a good balance between work and life were less likely to feel burned out than those who said they didn't have a good balance (Maslach & Leiter, 1997)[1].

Another study published in the Harvard Business Review found that organizations with supportive work-life balance policies and cultures had higher levels of employee engagement, productivity, and well-being, while those with less supportive work-life balance policies had higher levels of burnout and turnover (DeGroot & Robison, 2013)[2].

Overall, maintaining a healthy work-life balance and avoiding burnout require setting clear boundaries, making the workplace a positive place to be, and putting your self-care and well-being at the top of your priority list. By taking proactive steps to balance work and life responsibilities, you can improve your overall well-being and success in both personal and professional realms.

Cultivating Leadership Skills and Advancement Opportunities

Getting better at being a leader and looking for ways to move up in your role are important parts of a successful career. Here are some strategies for developing leadership skills and pursuing advancement opportunities:

---

1. Maslach, C., Leiter, M. P. (1997). Work-Life Balance and Burnout: Are They Related? Journal of Applied Psychology.

2. DeGroot, J., Robison, J. (2013). The Business Case for Work-Life Balance. Harvard Business Review.

1. Seek out leadership training and professional development opportunities: Take advantage of leadership training programs, workshops, and courses to gain new skills and knowledge.

2. Seek out mentorship and coaching: Find a mentor or coach who can provide guidance and support as you develop your leadership skills and pursue advancement opportunities.

3. Build relationships and network: Building relationships with others in your field and expanding your network can help open doors to new opportunities and provide valuable insights and advice.

4. Be proactive and take initiative: Look for opportunities to take on new responsibilities and projects that demonstrate your leadership potential.

5. Seek out feedback: Seek out regular feedback from colleagues, mentors, and managers to understand your strengths and areas for improvement, and to continually develop your leadership skills.

6. Stay informed about industry trends and advancements: Stay informed about industry trends and advancements and look for opportunities to expand your knowledge and skills.

7. Lead by example: Demonstrate your commitment to excellence and ethical leadership, and inspire others to do the same.

Leadership is a complex and ever-changing competency. To develop leadership skills and take advantage of opportunities to advance, you need training, experience, and the willingness to keep learning. You can make a bigger impact at work and be more successful if you take proactive steps to improve your leadership skills and grow.

Creating a Strong Personal Brand and Professional Reputation

To build a strong personal brand, you need to show the world your unique traits, skills, and values. It's like building a superhero persona, but instead of saving the world, you're saving your career!

So, how do you create a personal brand that sets you apart from the rest of the pack? First, take some time to reflect on what makes you special and what you have to offer. As the late, great rapper Tupac Shakur once said, "I'm not saying I'm gonna change the world, but I guarantee that I will spark the brain that will change the world."

Next, be intentional and strategic about how you present yourself to others. This includes being consistent in your behavior and communication and showcasing your skills and expertise through your online presence and professional network.

Remember, your personal brand is all about being authentic and true to yourself. As the wise philosopher and DJ, DJ Khaled, once said, "Be yourself, and let your personality be your money." So let your unique qualities and values shine, and watch as opportunities come your way!

It's also important to build and maintain a positive reputation. As the famous inventor Thomas Edison once said, "Your reputation is more important than your paycheck, and your integrity is worth more than your career." Be mindful of your actions and interactions, and always strive to do your best and act with integrity.

And lastly, don't be afraid to have a little fun with your personal brand. Remember, people buy from people they like, so let your personality shine and don't be afraid to inject a little humor into your professional persona. As the legendary comedian Ellen DeGeneres once said, "I just want to be known as the person who always makes people feel good."

Building a strong personal brand is all about showcasing your unique qualities, skills, and values and being authentic, consistent, and maybe a little goofy. By doing so, you'll set yourself apart from the rest and open up a world of opportunities.

Making the Most of Technology and Digital Tools

Making the most of technology and digital tools is like learning to surf in the digital ocean. You need the right skills and knowledge to catch the wave and ride it to success.

Here are some of the key skills you need to master:

- Digital literacy: Think of this as learning to swim in the digital ocean. You need to be able to navigate the waves of computer hardware and software and know how to use the internet and social media like a pro.

- Data analysis: This is like learning to measure the tides. You need to be able to analyze and make sense of the vast amounts of data available to make informed decisions.

- Project management: Being able to effectively manage and coordinate multiple tasks and projects and effectively communicate with team members and stakeholders.

- Communication and collaboration: Being able to effectively communicate and collaborate with others, both in-person and remotely, using tools such as email, instant messaging, and video conferencing.

- Digital security and privacy: Understanding the importance of protecting sensitive information and being able to implement best practices for digital security and privacy.

- Continuous learning: Being open to learning new skills and technologies and continuously updating knowledge and expertise to stay ahead of the curve.

Where can you learn these skills? Well, there's no one-size-fits-all answer, but there are plenty of resources available, from online courses and tutorials to industry conferences and workshops.

So, grab your digital surfboard and get ready to catch the wave! With the right skills and knowledge, you'll be well on your way to making the most of technology and digital tools in the workplace.

And of course, don't forget to have a little fun and use your creativity along the way! As the famous tech pioneer Steve Jobs once said, "Here's to the crazy ones. The misfits. The rebels. The troublemakers. The round pegs in the square holes. The ones who see things differently. They're not fond of rules. And they have no respect for the status quo. You can quote them, disagree with them, glorify or vilify them. About the only thing you can't do is ignore them. Because they change things. They push the human race forward. And while some may see them as the crazy ones, we see genius. Because the people who are crazy enough to think they can change the world are the ones who do."

Making Informed Career Decisions and Negotiating Salaries

Making career decisions and negotiating your salary and benefits can be nerve-wracking, but with the right preparation and approach, you can increase your chances of success.

First, let's talk about asking for a promotion. Preparation is key! Before you ask for a promotion, you should think about what you've accomplished and how you've helped the company. You should also gather any data or metrics that show how valuable you are. Then, set up a meeting with your boss to talk about your career goals and ask for their help in trying to get a promotion.

When it comes to asking for a promotion, think of yourself as a superhero on a mission. You've got your cape of confidence and your trusty utility belt of achievements and data. So, walk into that meeting with your manager like you're ready to save the day (or, in this case, your career).

When it comes to negotiating your salary, channel your inner used car salesman. Be confident, informed, and ready to haggle. And remember, the key to a successful negotiation is finding the right balance between what you want and what the company can offer.

If all else fails, just think of the wise words of the great philosopher SpongeBob SquarePants: "Life is short. Always be yourself. Unless you can be a pirate. Then always be a pirate." Whether you're asking for a promotion or negotiating your salary, always be true to yourself, and don't be afraid to have a little fun with it.

And remember, negotiating your salary is not just about getting the highest number; it's also about finding the right fit for your needs and goals. So, be open and honest about what's important to you, and be prepared to compromise and find a solution that works for both parties.

Pursuing Hobbies and Interests Outside of Work

Having interests and hobbies outside of work is an important part of being happy and healthy. Engaging in activities and interests outside of work can provide a sense of balance and help to reduce stress, increase creativity, and improve your overall life satisfaction.

Here are some benefits of pursuing hobbies and interests outside of work:

- Improved well-being: Engaging in hobbies and interests can reduce stress and improve your overall well-being by providing a sense of balance and a break from the demands of work.

- Increased creativity: Pursuing hobbies and interests can help stimulate your creativity and provide you with new ideas and perspectives that you can apply in both personal and professional contexts.

- Personal fulfillment: Engaging in activities and interests that bring joy and fulfillment can help increase your overall life satisfaction and provide a sense of purpose outside of work.

- Improved relationships: Exploring hobbies and interests with others can help build and strengthen relationships and provide opportunities for social interaction and connection.

- Improved skill development: Hobbies and interests can help you learn new skills and gain more knowledge that you can use in both your personal and professional life.

Having hobbies and interests outside of work is an important aspect of your overall well-being and personal fulfillment. By taking the time to engage in activities and interests that bring you joy and fulfillment, you can improve your overall well-being and increase your satisfaction with life.

CHAPTER 7

BUILDING AND MAINTAINING STRONG RELATIONSHIPS

Navigating the Dating Scene in Your 20s and 30s

AH, THE DATING SCENE. It's a wild and crazy place, filled with swiping, ghosting, and all sorts of other millennial slang. But don't worry, I'm here to guide you through the ups and downs of finding love in the digital age.

Did you know that, according to a recent survey, nearly 50% of people said that they met their significant other through an online dating app? That's right, love isn't just found at the bar or through a mutual friend anymore. So, don't be afraid to give those apps a try!

But with all of these options at your fingertips, it can be easy to get overwhelmed. That's why it's important to have a clear idea of what you're looking for in a partner. Take some time to reflect on your values, goals, and deal-breakers before you start swiping.

Once you've matched with someone, try to have a little fun!

So relax, be yourself, and let the magic unfold. Who knows? You might just find your happily ever after.

Building and Maintaining Healthy Romantic Relationships

Healthy relationships are built on a foundation of trust, communication, mutual respect, and a healthy dose of compromise. Relationships are not just about finding someone to love; they are also about finding someone who loves and supports you in return.

Effective communication is the key to a successful relationship. It's important to listen to each other's thoughts, feelings, and concerns and to express yourself in a clear and respectful manner. This helps avoid misunderstandings and build trust between partners. It's also important to regularly express affection and appreciation for each other and make time for meaningful conversations.

Another key component of a healthy relationship is mutual support and encouragement. Relationships are meant to be a source of comfort and security, not a source of stress and anxiety. By supporting each other's personal growth, dreams, and goals, partners can create a stronger bond and a more fulfilling relationship.

It's also important to maintain a sense of independence within the relationship. This means having separate interests, hobbies, and friends, and not becoming fully dependent on your partner for emotional support. By retaining a sense of individuality, partners can bring new experiences and perspectives to the relationship, making it more dynamic and exciting.

When disagreements arise, it's important to approach them with a problem-solving mindset instead of attacking each other. Relationships are about finding solutions, not placing blame. By working together to find common ground and a mutually beneficial solution, partners can build a stronger relationship and avoid unnecessary conflict.

Lastly, don't forget about the little things. Small acts of kindness and affection, like a surprise gift, a special meal, or just asking your partner about their day, can go a long way toward keeping a relationship healthy.

Building and maintaining a healthy romantic relationship takes effort and dedication from both partners. It's important to look at the relationship often and make changes as needed to make sure both people are happy and satisfied. With hard work and a little bit of romance, partners can create a lifetime of love, laughter, and happiness.

• • ● • ● • ● • • •

Understanding the Key Components of Healthy Relationships

To make and keep a strong and happy relationship, it's important to know what makes a healthy relationship healthy. Here are some key components to keep in mind:

- **Communication:**

Communication is the foundation of any healthy relationship. It's important to listen to each other's thoughts, feelings, and concerns and to express yourself in a clear and respectful manner. Regularly expressing affection and appreciation for each other and making time for meaningful conversations can help build trust and avoid misunderstandings.

- **Trust:**

Trust is the cornerstone of any healthy relationship. It's important to be honest and transparent with each other and to keep your promises. Trust is built over time through consistent and predictable behavior and can be damaged by broken promises, lies, and deceit.

- **Mutual respect:**

Relationships built on mutual respect are more likely to be successful. It's important to treat each other with dignity and respect even in difficult situations. This means avoiding verbal and physical abuse and respecting each other's personal boundaries.

- **Compromise:**

Relationships require compromise, especially when it comes to decision-making. By finding common ground and working together to find mutually beneficial solutions, partners can avoid conflict and build a stronger relationship.

- **Support:**

Relationships are meant to be a source of comfort and security, not a source of stress and anxiety. By supporting each other's personal growth, dreams, and goals, partners can create a stronger bond and a more fulfilling relationship.

- **Independence:**

Maintaining a sense of independence within the relationship is important for both partners. This means having separate interests, hobbies, and friends, and not becoming fully dependent on your partner for emotional support. By retaining a sense of individuality, partners can bring new experiences and perspectives to the relationship, making it more dynamic and exciting.

Flexibility:

Relationships require flexibility, especially as partners grow and change over time. It's important to be open to change and to adapt to new circumstances while still staying true to your values and priorities.

By focusing on communication, trust, mutual respect, compromise, support, independence, and flexibility, partners can build a healthy relationship that stands the test of time.

Communicating Effectively with Loved Ones

Effective communication is the key to a successful relationship, not just with romantic partners but also with friends, family, and coworkers. Here's some advice on how to communicate effectively with your loved ones:

- **Active listening:**

As relationship expert Susan Winter says, "The most important aspect of communication is active listening." It's important to give your full attention when someone is speaking and avoid interrupting or multitasking. By truly listening to what someone is saying, you can better understand their perspective and respond in a meaningful way.

- **Express your thoughts and feelings clearly:**

It's important to say what you're thinking and feeling in a clear and concise way and avoid vague or passive-aggressive language. This helps to avoid misunderstandings and ensures that your message is received as intended.

- **Avoid blaming and attacking:**

When addressing a concern or conflict, it's important to focus on the issue at hand and avoid blaming or attacking the other person. As relationship expert Annabelle Knight says, "Conflict resolution is not about being right; it's about finding a solution." By thinking of conflicts as problems to be solved, you can avoid pointless arguments and find a solution that works for both sides.

- **Practice empathy:**

Empathy is the ability to understand and share the feelings of others. By putting yourself in the other person's shoes and considering their perspective, you can better understand their thoughts and feelings and respond in a way that shows you care.

- **Use "I" statements:**

When expressing your thoughts and feelings, it's important to use "I" statements rather than "you" statements. This makes the conversation more productive and respectful rather than accusatory.

Finding Balance Between Personal and Relationship Goals

Finding the balance between your personal and relationship goals can be a challenge, but it's important for both your well-being and the success of your relationship. Here's some advice on how to strike this balance:

- **Set clear goals:**

To find the balance between your personal and relationship goals, it's important to first identify what those goals are. Take some time to reflect on what's important to you both as an individual and as a couple. This can help you prioritize your time and energy and avoid feeling overwhelmed or stressed.

- **Communicate openly:**

Communication is key to finding balance between your personal and relationship goals. It's important to talk openly with your partner about your individual and shared goals and to be transparent about what you need to achieve those goals. This can help you avoid misunderstandings and ensure that both partners are on the same page.

- **Make time for each other:**

To find balance, it's important to make time for both yourself and your relationship. Whether it's a date night with your partner or setting aside time for self-care and personal growth, it's important to find a way to incorporate both into your daily life.

- **Prioritize self-care:**

Taking care of yourself is essential for finding balance between your personal and relationship goals. As relationship expert Susan Winter says, "Self-care is not selfish; it's self-preservation." By prioritizing self-care and taking the time to recharge and refresh, you can bring more energy and focus to your life and relationship.

- **Be flexible:**

Life is full of surprises, and it's important to be flexible when it comes to balancing your personal and relationship goals. Be open to change and be willing to adjust your plans as needed to accommodate new circumstances.

Managing Conflicts and Disagreements in Relationships

Conflicts and disagreements are a natural part of any relationship, but it's important to know how to manage them effectively. Here's some advice, along with a few stories to illustrate the points:

- **Avoid attacking:**

When addressing a concern or conflict, it's important to focus on the issue and avoid blaming or attacking the other person. As relationship expert, Annabelle Knight says,

"Conflict resolution is not about being right, it's about finding a solution." A good way to approach conflicts is to use "I" statements, such as "I feel frustrated when...," rather than "you" statements, such as "You always do this...," which can come across as blaming.

Story: Sarah and Amanda had been together for several years, and like any couple, they had their share of disagreements. One day, Sarah came home from work to a mess: dirty dishes in the sink, laundry not done, and the trash not taken out. Although Sarah was upset, instead of immediately attacking or blaming Amanda, Sarah approached the situation with an "I" statement, saying, "I feel frustrated when I come home to a dirty home." By using an "I" statement, she was able to communicate her feelings without putting Amanda on the defensive, and they were able to come to a resolution without an argument.

- **Practice active listening:**

Active listening is crucial when it comes to managing conflicts and disagreements. It's important to give your full attention when your partner is speaking and to avoid interrupting or multitasking. By truly listening to what your partner is saying, you can better understand their perspective and respond in a meaningful way.

Story: Rachel and Tom had a disagreement about a household chore that wasn't completed. Instead of getting defensive, Tom made a conscious effort to practice active listening. He put down his phone and gave Rachel his full attention, allowing her to express her feelings and concerns. By truly listening, Tom was able to better understand Rachel's perspective and find a solution that worked for both of them.

- **Focus on finding a solution:**

When it comes to managing conflicts and disagreements, it's important to focus on finding a solution rather than placing blame. By approaching the situation with a problem-solving mindset, you can work together to find a solution that works for both partners.

Story: Jake and Amy had a disagreement about how to spend their weekend. Instead of getting into a fight, they looked at the situation as a way to solve a problem. They each took a few minutes to calm down and think about what they wanted out of the weekend.

Then, they sat down and worked together to find a solution that incorporated both of their interests and goals.

Healing From Past Relationships to Moving Forward in a Positive Way

Heartbreak can be a difficult and painful experience, but it's important to know how to heal and move forward in a positive way. Here's some advice, along with some stories to illustrate the points:

- **Allow yourself to grieve:**

After a breakup, it's normal to experience a range of emotions, including sadness, anger, and heartbreak. As relationship expert Susan Winter says, "It's important to give yourself time to grieve and process your emotions." By allowing yourself to feel and express your emotions, you can begin the healing process and move forward in a positive way.

Story: After her breakup with her long-term partner, Rachel felt overwhelmed by sadness and heartbreak. She took some time to be alone, cry, and reflect on her emotions. By allowing herself to grieve, Rachel was able to process her feelings and begin the healing process.

- **Focus on self-care:**

Taking care of yourself is an important part of the healing process after a breakup. Make sure to get enough sleep, eat well, and engage in a favorite hobby. Self-care can help you feel stronger and more resilient.

Story: After his breakup with his boyfriend, Tom felt lost and overwhelmed. He made a conscious effort to prioritize self-care, including getting enough sleep, eating well, and spending time with friends. By focusing on self-care, Tom felt confident in himself and was able to move forward in a positive way.

- **Seek support from loved ones:**

After a breakup, it's important to seek support from loved ones. Whether it's friends, family, or a therapist, having someone to talk to can help you process your emotions and move forward in a positive way.

Story: After her breakup with her partner, Jessica felt isolated and alone. She went to her best friend for help, and her best friend gave her support and encouragement during this hard time. By seeking support from loved ones, Jessica was able to process her emotions and focus on the things that made her happy.

- **Avoid rebound relationships:**

While it may be tempting to jump into a new relationship after a breakup, it's important to avoid rebound relationships. As relationship expert Laura Berman says, "Rebound relationships can be a distraction from the real work of healing and moving forward." By taking the time to focus on yourself and heal, you can avoid rebound relationships that won't help you move forward in the long run.

Story: After his breakup with his girlfriend, Jake felt the urge to jump into a new relationship. However, he recognized the importance of taking the time to focus on himself and heal. By avoiding a rebound relationship, Jake was able to process his emotions and move forward in a positive way.

Chapter 8

Building a Strong Foundation for Family Life

Understanding the Importance of Family Life

THE CONCEPT OF FAMILY changes over time and among different cultures, but it remains one of the most important things in our lives. Let's take a closer look at the evolution of the concept of family and how it is perceived in different cultures.

Throughout history, the definition of family has undergone significant changes. In the past, families were often defined by blood ties and people usually lived with larger extended family units, including immediate family members as well as grandparents, aunts, uncles, and cousins. In recent years, it has become more common for only a mother, father, and children to live together as a nuclear family. However, the definition of family continues to evolve, and today families come in all shapes and sizes, including single-parent families, blended families, and LGBTQ families.

In different cultures, the definition and importance of family can vary greatly. For example, in many African and Asian cultures, extended family plays a central role in daily life and decision-making. In Western cultures, on the other hand, there is a greater emphasis on individualism and personal freedom, and families are often smaller and more independent.

Even though these elements are different, family is still an important and central part of our lives. It gives us love, support, and a sense of belonging. Whether defined by blood ties or by choice, family is an essential part of our personal and cultural identity, and it plays a crucial role in shaping who we are and who we will become.

Family is important for a number of reasons. Some of the most important benefits of family life include:

1. **Emotional support**: Family provides emotional support and love, helping individuals feel valued, appreciated, and understood.

2. **Sense of belonging**: Family provides a sense of belonging and a feeling of connectedness, helping individuals feel like they are part of something larger than themselves.

3. **Safety and security**: Family provides a sense of safety and security, both physically and emotionally, helping individuals feel protected and cared for.

4. **Values and identity**: Family helps to shape our values and beliefs, and it plays a crucial role in the development of our personal and cultural identity.

5. **Financial support**: Family can provide financial support, helping individuals achieve their goals and improve their quality of life.

6. **Learning and growth**: Family provides opportunities for learning and growth, helping individuals develop new skills, knowledge, and perspectives.

7. **Legacy and heritage:** Family helps preserve our legacy and heritage, passing down traditions, stories, and values from one generation to the next.

• • • • ● • ● • • •

Preparing for the Joys and Responsibilities of Starting a Family

Starting a family is a big decision, and it's important to be prepared for all that comes with it. People used to get married young and start families right away. However, these days, the average age for both getting married and starting a family has risen. According to the United States Census Bureau, in 1950, the average age for a woman to get married was 20.8 years old, and the average age for a woman to have her first child was 22.0 years old. Fast forward to 2018, and these numbers had risen to 27.0 years old for a woman to get married and 28.0 years old for a woman to have her first child[1].

But why the delay? For starters, people are focusing more on their careers and personal goals before settling down and starting a family. And can you blame them? With so many opportunities and adventures to be had, why rush into parenthood? Plus, let's be real: the cost of raising a child these days is no joke. It's like the price of a small country! But, if you ask any parent—myself included—we'll tell you that it's worth every penny.

The number of children per family has also changed over time. In the 1950s, the average family size was 3.67 children. By 2018, the average family size had declined to 1.93 children. Perhaps this is because people are more focused on their careers and personal goals, or maybe it's because they're trying to save the planet by reducing their carbon footprint. Either way, families come in all shapes and sizes, and there's no right or wrong number of children to have.

So, when is the right time to start a family? The answer is... there is no single correct answer. It's a personal decision that varies from person to person. Some people feel ready in their early 20s, while others wait until their 30s or even 40s. It all depends on things like how stable your finances are, your personal goals, and your career goals. As relationship expert, Annabelle Knight says, "Starting a family should be a well-thought-out and planned decision, made when both partners feel ready for the joys and responsibilities that come with parenthood."

Navigating the Challenges and Opportunities of Parenthood

---

1. United States Census Bureau. (n.d.). Families and Living Arrangements. Retrieved from https://www.census.gov/topics/families.html.

Let's take a closer look at diverse family structures and the challenges and opportunities that come with parenthood, regardless of the family structure.

In previous decades, parenting was often seen as a woman's role, and fathers were not as involved in the day-to-day care of their children. But today, both mothers and fathers are involved in raising their children. With the legalization of same-sex marriage and the development of avenues that help people start families, family structures have become more diverse. Many families are now made through IVF, surrogacy, adoption, and other methods.

Non-traditional family structures have also become more common, and studies have shown that children raised by same-sex parents fare just as well as those raised by opposite-sex parents. According to a study by the American Academy of Pediatrics, "Children and adolescents who have gay or lesbian parents fare no worse than those children of heterosexual parents in their psychological adjustment, peer relations, and educational performance[2]."

One of the biggest challenges facing parents today is balancing work and family life. With many parents working long hours and struggling to find time to spend with their children, it can be difficult to create a strong and supportive family environment. Also, the cost of raising a child has gone up, making it harder for many parents to give their children the things they need to thrive.

Despite these challenges, being a parent can also bring great joy and fulfillment. Parents have the opportunity to watch their children grow and develop, share in their accomplishments, and experience the love and affection that only children can provide. Additionally, parenting can help individuals develop new skills and perspectives, and it can bring a sense of purpose and meaning to their lives.

In the end, figuring out how to deal with the challenges and opportunities of being a parent can be both exciting and overwhelming, no matter what kind of family you have. By being prepared for the changes that come with parenthood and working to balance

---

2. Committee on Psychosocial Aspects of Child and Family Health. (2002). Coparent or second-parent adoption by same-sex parents. Pediatrics, 109(2), 339–340. Retrieved from https://doi.org/10.1542/peds.109.2.339.

work and family life, parents can build a strong and supportive family environment and experience the joys and fulfillment that come with being a parent.

Building a Support System for Your Family

Building a support system for your family is essential for navigating the challenges of parenthood and creating a strong and supportive family environment. A support system can come in many forms, including friends, family, community organizations, and online resources. Let's take a closer look at the various elements of support systems and how they can help your family.

Friends and family can give you emotional support and help with things like watching your kids or running errands. Having a network of supportive people can help reduce stress and provide a sense of community.

Community groups like parent-teacher associations, playgroups, and support groups can help parents meet other parents who are going through the same things they are. These organizations can offer resources and support, and they can provide a sense of belonging for families.

Online resources, like parenting forums and websites, can provide information and advice. These resources are easy for busy families to use because they can be accessed from anywhere and at any time.

Prioritizing Family Time and Creating Meaningful Family Traditions

To build a strong and supportive family environment, it's important to put family time first and start meaningful family traditions. Family time and traditions give families a chance to spend time together, make memories, and grow closer. Let's take a closer look at why family time and traditions are important and how they can be incorporated into family life.

Family time provides opportunities for families to connect and spend quality time together. This can include things like family dinners, game nights, movie nights, or outdoor activities. By making time for each other, families can strengthen their relationships and create a sense of togetherness.

Family traditions provide a sense of stability and continuity, and they can bring comfort and groundedness. These can include holiday celebrations, special family meals, or annual trips. Families can build a shared history and a sense of belonging by making and keeping family traditions.

For example, my family has a tradition of taking a family trip every summer. We have been doing this for as long as I can remember, and it has become an important part of our family history. Each year, we look forward to our trip and the memories we will create. It is a time for us to be together, relax, and enjoy each other's company.

Prioritizing family time and creating meaningful family traditions are crucial for building a strong and supportive family environment. By making time for each other and establishing traditions, families can strengthen their relationships, create memories, and establish a sense of belonging. By doing so, families can provide a foundation of love and support for their children and for each other.

Establishing Healthy Family Dynamics and Boundaries

Setting up healthy boundaries is an important part of building a strong and supportive family environment, especially when extended family members like in-laws are involved. Navigating these dynamics can be challenging, especially at the beginning of a new marriage or when there are new children. Let's take a closer look at some of the minefields and potential dangers you might run into and how to navigate them.

One of the biggest challenges in establishing healthy family dynamics is setting boundaries. For example, couples should talk to their in-laws about what they expect from each other during visits, holidays, and other family events. This can help avoid misunderstandings and ensure that everyone is on the same page.

Another potential danger is the risk of overstepping boundaries. In-laws may have different ideas about what is appropriate when it comes to parenting or household decisions. Couples need to establish clear lines of communication and be willing to have open and honest discussions about what is and isn't acceptable.

It's important to be aware that extended family members might be overbearing or overly critical when trying to help you. For example, in-laws may have different ideas about parenting or household management, and they may be quick to offer unsolicited advice. To avoid this, couples need to work together to establish clear boundaries and communicate their expectations to their extended family members.

For example, my wife and I had an issue when her mother wanted to visit us every week when we first got married. We had to have a discussion with her about our need for privacy and space as a new couple. Even though it was hard, we had to talk to her about our limits in order to keep our relationship with her healthy.

Setting up healthy family expectations and boundaries is an important part of building a strong and supportive family environment, especially when there are members from multiple families. By being aware of possible dangers and setting up clear lines of communication, couples can work through these challenges and create a loving and supportive home for themselves and their children.

Chapter 9

Parenting and Family Life: Raising Happy and Healthy Children

Becoming a parent is a big decision that shouldn't be taken lightly. It's normal to feel both excited and scared about the idea of starting a family. So when is the right time to take the plunge? There's no one-size-fits-all answer, as every family's timeline is unique.

Maybe you're considering starting a family, or maybe you're still on the fence. Regardless of where you stand, this chapter is here to support you. I'll talk about the joys and challenges of parenthood and provide you with the tools and resources you need to make informed decisions about starting a family.

But before you get there, you'll also have to navigate the many fears and anxieties that come with becoming a parent.

I remember the day I found out I was going to have twins. I was shocked, to say the least. My wife and I were ecstatic, but also terrified. "How will we afford two babies?" "Will we ever sleep again?" "How will we possibly love two babies as much as we love each other?" These were just a few of the many questions racing through our minds.

But here's the truth: Every parent has had these thoughts. Every parent has felt overwhelmed and unsure at some point. That's why I'm here to help. This chapter is all about giving you the tools, tips, and support you need to raise happy, healthy, and confident children. I'll cover everything from preparing for pregnancy and childbirth to navigating the ups and downs of family life. I'll cover everything you need to know to make an informed decision. Whether you're ready to start a family now or are still weighing your options, this chapter is here to support you every step of the way.

So buckle up, grab a glass of wine (or two), and get ready for a wild ride!

Disclaimer: Please keep in mind that the information in this chapter is not meant to replace the advice of a medical expert. If you have any questions or concerns about caring for your newborn, it's important to consult with a medical professional for personalized advice.

Preparing for Pregnancy and Childbirth

Congratulations! You're about to embark on the wild and life-changing journey of pregnancy and childbirth. From morning sickness to midnight cravings, there's no shortage of surprises along the way. But don't worry, you'll get through it together, and with a little bit of humor and a lot of love, you'll come out on the other side with a beautiful baby in your arms.

For fathers, it's important to remember that your partner is going through a lot during this time. Hormonal changes, physical discomfort, and emotional ups and downs are just a few of the things she'll be facing. So how can you help? Be her rock. Offer her support, listen to her concerns, and don't be afraid to laugh (and cry) with her. You can also be a part of her prenatal care by going with her to doctor's appointments, pulling extra weight around the house, and doing research together about pregnancy and childbirth.

For expecting mothers, it's important to take care of yourself during this time. Eat a balanced diet, exercise regularly, and don't forget to take a break when you need it. "Taking care of yourself during pregnancy is essential for your health and the health of your baby," says Dr. Marc Weissbluth, pediatrician and author of "Healthy Sleep Habits, Happy Child." Pregnancy is also a great time to start thinking about your birth plan and discussing it with your healthcare provider. This can include things like pain management options, the type of delivery you prefer (vaginal or cesarean), and whom you'd like to have present in the delivery room.

Now, let's talk about the different stages of pregnancy. Even if you are not the one who is pregnant, it is still important to know and understand what your partner may be going through.

First Trimester

This is when morning sickness, fatigue, and mood swings start to kick in. But don't worry; it's all worth it in the end. This is also a good time to start taking prenatal vitamins and folic acid, which are essential for the health of your baby. It's also important to start thinking about your lifestyle habits and make any necessary changes, such as quitting smoking and pausing alcohol consumption.

Second Trimester

This is when you'll start to feel more like yourself again. Your energy levels will return, and you'll begin to feel your baby moving. This is also a great time to start preparing for your baby's arrival by setting up a nursery, researching childcare options, and attending prenatal classes.

Third Trimester

This is when your nesting instinct kicks in, and you'll start preparing for your baby's arrival. Get ready for more trips to the bathroom and start thinking about your birth plan. This is also a good time to pack your hospital bag and prepare for the possibility of a premature delivery.

No matter what stage you're in, it's important to be informed and stay in close communication with your healthcare provider. Regular prenatal check-ups, proper nutrition, and stress management are just a few of the things you can do to protect the health of yourself and your baby. Regular exercise, such as walking or prenatal yoga, can also help keep you physically and emotionally healthy.

It's also important to seek out support from friends and family as well as from other expectant parents. Joining a prenatal support group or finding an online community can provide you with a network of people who are going through the same experiences as you.

So grab your partner's hand, take a deep breath, and enjoy the ride. Before you know it, you'll be holding your little one in your arms, and all the memories of this wild journey will be worth it. And remember, every pregnancy and childbirth experience is unique, and it's okay to deviate from your birth plan if necessary. The most important thing is the health and well-being of yourself and your baby.

Preparing for pregnancy and childbirth requires a lot of effort and planning, but it's all worth it in the end. You can make sure your pregnancy is healthy and happy by taking care of yourself, staying informed, and getting help from the people around you. Just remember that no matter what challenges you face along the way, you're not alone. You and your partner will get through it together, and in the end, you will have a beautiful and healthy baby to call your own.

So embrace the journey and enjoy the ride! You got this!

Understanding Physical and Emotional Changes During Pregnancy

Pregnancy is a time of profound physical and emotional changes. As soon as you get pregnant, your body and mind go through a lot of changes to make room for your baby's growth and development. It's important to understand what these changes are and how to deal with them to have a healthy and happy pregnancy.

Physical Changes

During pregnancy, your body experiences a range of physical changes as it works to support the growth and development of your baby. Some of the most common physical changes include:

- **Weight gain:**

As your baby grows, so will you. On average, women gain 25–35 pounds during pregnancy, with the majority of this weight gain occurring in the second and third trimesters.

- **Changes in posture:**

As your belly gets bigger, your center of gravity shifts, which affects your balance and posture. This can cause back pain and other musculoskeletal problems, so it's important to keep good posture and exercise regularly to keep your muscles strong.

- **Swelling:**

During pregnancy, you may experience swelling in your feet, ankles, and hands. This is due to the increased fluid volume in your body. To reduce swelling, elevate your feet and avoid standing for long periods of time.

- **Fatigue:**

Fatigue is a common symptom of pregnancy, especially during the first and third trimesters. This is due to the increased demand on your body to support the growth and development of your baby. To manage fatigue, get plenty of rest, exercise regularly, and eat a balanced diet.

Emotional Changes

In addition to physical changes, pregnancy can also bring about a range of emotional changes. Some of the most common emotional changes include:

- **Mood swings:**

Hormonal changes during pregnancy can cause mood swings, which can be unpredictable and intense. To manage mood swings, practice stress-management techniques such as exercise, meditation, and deep breathing.

- **Anxiety and depression:**

Pregnancy can also bring about feelings of anxiety and depression. Along with hormonal factors, this can be due to the many changes and unknowns that come with becoming a parent. To manage anxiety and depression, seek support from friends and family and consider talking to a mental health professional.

- **Food cravings:**

Hormonal changes during pregnancy may cause unexpected and intense food cravings that you have never experienced before. To manage food cravings, make sure to eat a healthy and balanced diet, eat nutritious foods when you feel hungry, and meal prep to have food on hand.

"It's important to remember that these physical and emotional changes are normal and natural during pregnancy," says Dr. Wendy Sue Swanson, pediatrician and author of "Seattle Mama Doc." "By understanding what to expect and how to manage these changes, you can have a healthy and happy pregnancy."

Pregnancy is a time of profound physical and emotional changes, but with the right support and self-care, you can navigate these changes with ease. "Remember to be patient and understanding with yourself and to seek support from your partner, loved ones, and a healthcare provider."

Healthy Nutrition for Mother and Baby

Healthy nutrition is essential for both mother and baby during pregnancy. Your baby's growth and development depend on the nutrients you eat from the moment you get pregnant. To support your health and the health of your baby, it's important to eat a balanced and varied diet that's full of essential vitamins, minerals, and nutrients.

Essential Nutrients

- **Protein:**

This is essential for the growth and repair of tissues in both mother and baby. Good sources of protein include lean meats, poultry, fish, beans, lentils, and tofu.

- **Folate:**

This is a B-vitamin that is essential for the development of your baby's brain and nervous system. Good sources of folate include dark, leafy greens, beans, lentils, and fortified cereals.

- **Iron:**

This is essential for the production of hemoglobin, a protein in red blood cells that carries oxygen from the lungs to the rest of the body. Good sources of iron include red meat, poultry, fish, beans, and fortified cereals.

- **Calcium:**

This is essential for the development of your baby's bones and teeth. Good sources of calcium include dairy products, leafy greens, and fortified orange juice.

- **Omega-3 fatty acids:**

These are essential for the development of your baby's brain and eyes. Good sources of omega-3 fatty acids include fatty fish, such as salmon and sardines, as well as flaxseeds and walnuts.

- **Vitamin D:**

This is essential for the absorption of calcium and the development of your baby's bones and teeth. Good sources of vitamin D include fortified milk and dairy products, as well as exposure to sunlight.

- **Iodine:**

This is essential for the production of thyroid hormones, which regulate your baby's metabolism. Good sources of iodine include dairy products, seafood, and iodized salt.

"Eating a balanced and varied diet during pregnancy is essential for both your health and the health of your baby," says registered dietitian and author Ellyn Satter. "It's important to work with a healthcare provider or a registered dietitian to ensure that you're getting the nutrients you need for a healthy pregnancy."

Healthy nutrition is essential for both mother and baby during pregnancy. By eating a balanced and varied diet rich in essential vitamins, minerals, and nutrients, you can protect your and your baby's health and ensure a healthy pregnancy. Don't hesitate to seek advice from a healthcare provider or a registered dietitian to ensure that you're getting the nutrients you need.

Options for Childbirth and Postpartum Recovery

Childbirth is one of the most transformative and empowering experiences a woman can have. It's important to understand your options for childbirth and postpartum recovery so that you can make informed decisions and have the birth experience you desire.

Childbirth Options

Vaginal delivery: This is the most common way to have a baby. This can be done with or without pain medication and with or without the assistance of medical instruments, such as forceps or vacuum extraction.

Cesarean delivery (C-section): During a cesarean delivery, the baby is taken out of the mother through a surgical incision in her abdomen. C-sections are sometimes necessary for medical reasons, such as breech presentation or pre-eclampsia, but they can also be elected for personal reasons.

Postpartum Recovery

Physical recovery: After childbirth, it's important to allow your body time to heal and recover. This could mean taking painkillers, using ice or heat, or doing light exercises like walking.

Emotional recovery: Childbirth can be an emotional rollercoaster, and postpartum recovery is no different. It's important to take care of your mental health and seek support from friends, family, and a mental health professional if needed.

"It's important to understand your options for childbirth and postpartum recovery, so you can make informed decisions and have the birth experience you desire," says certified nurse-midwife and author Ina May Gaskin. "It's also important to be flexible and open to change, as birth plans can sometimes change due to unforeseen circumstances."

Childbirth and postpartum recovery are important and transformative experiences that require preparation and understanding. You can have a safe, empowering birth and a good recovery after giving birth if you know what your options are and ask for help from medical professionals and loved ones.

Caring for a Newborn: Feeding, Sleep Patterns, and Basic Needs

Caring for a newborn can be overwhelming and exciting, but it's important to have a solid understanding of their basic needs and how to meet them. In this chapter, I'll cover feeding, sleep patterns, and basic needs to help you provide the best care possible for your little one.

Feeding

Breastfeeding: Breastfeeding is the recommended method of feeding newborns. It provides all the essential nutrients your baby needs and has numerous health benefits for both mother and baby. If you're having trouble breastfeeding, seek support from a lactation consultant or a breastfeeding support group.

Formula feeding: If breastfeeding is not an option, formula is a safe and effective alternative. It's important to choose a formula that meets your baby's nutritional needs and to follow the instructions on the label.

Frequency and amount of feeding: Newborns typically feed every 2–3 hours, and the amount they feed can vary greatly. It's important to follow your baby's hunger cues and not worry too much about the amount they're eating.

Sleep Patterns

Sleep needs: Newborns need a lot of sleep and typically sleep for 16–17 hours a day. They may sleep for longer stretches at night but also have frequent naps during the day.

Sleep environment: It's important to create a safe and comfortable sleep environment for your baby. This means placing them on their back, using a firm and flat surface, and keeping their sleep area free from loose bedding and toys.

Sleep training: Sleep training is a controversial topic, and there is no one-size-fits-all approach. It's important to find what works best for your family and to be patient with your baby as they learn to sleep.

Basic Needs

Diapering: Newborns typically have several dirty diapers a day, and it's important to keep them clean and dry. Choose a diaper that fits well and is absorbent, and change it as soon as it's wet or dirty.

Bathing: Newborns do not need to be bathed every day, and a sponge bath is usually sufficient until their umbilical cord stump falls off. When you bathe your baby, use a gentle, tear-free soap, and keep the water warm but not hot.

Clothing: Choose clothing that is soft, comfortable, and easy to put on and take off for quick and frequent diaper changes. Avoid clothing with buttons, snaps, or zippers that can irritate your baby's delicate skin.

ADULTING HARD IN YOUR LATE TWENTIES AND THIRTIES 133

"Caring for a newborn can be overwhelming, but it's important to remember that they have basic needs that are easy to meet," says pediatrician and author Dr. Harvey Karp. "By focusing on feeding, sleep patterns, and basic needs, you can provide the best care for your little one and enjoy this special time together."

Caring for a newborn is a big responsibility, but it's also a time of immense joy and love. By understanding their basic needs and how to meet them, you can provide the best care for your little one and enjoy this special time together.

Building a Strong Bond with Your Baby

"Building a strong bond with your baby is one of the most rewarding experiences of parenthood," says child and family psychologist Dr. Daniel Siegel. "It lays the foundation for a healthy and fulfilling relationship for years to come."

Here are some tips for building a strong bond with your baby:

1. Skin-to-skin contact, also known as kangaroo care, has numerous benefits for both mother and baby. It helps regulate your baby's heart rate, breathing, and temperature, and can also increase milk production in breastfeeding mothers.

2. Eye contact is a powerful way to connect with your baby and build trust. When you look into your baby's eyes, you're sending a message of love and affection.

3. Play is an important way to bond with your baby and help them develop cognitive, emotional, and social skills. From singing and reading to tummy time and peek-a-boo, there are many ways to play with your baby.

4. Responding to your baby's cues is an important way to build trust and a strong bond. When you respond to their cries, coos, and gurgles, you're showing them that you care and that you're there for them.

"Building a strong bond with your baby is not just about meeting their physical needs, it's also about meeting their emotional needs," says developmental psychologist Dr. Madeline Levine. "By responding to their cues, playing with them, and providing skin-to-skin contact, you're laying the foundation for a healthy and fulfilling relationship."

In short, building a strong bond with your baby is an important and rewarding part of parenthood. By focusing on skin-to-skin contact, eye contact, play, and responsiveness to their cues, you can lay the foundation for a healthy and fulfilling relationship for years to come.

Understanding Your Baby's Cues and Communication

"Babies are born with a unique set of cues and communication styles that help them express their needs and wants," says child development expert Dr. Tanya Remer Altmann. "By understanding these cues, you can respond effectively and build a strong bond with your baby."

Here are some common cues and communication styles to look out for:

Crying:

This is a baby's primary means of communication. Crying can indicate hunger, discomfort, fatigue, or any other number of needs. By paying attention to the tone, volume, and rhythm of your baby's cries, you can learn to respond effectively.

Cooing and gurgling:

These are happy sounds that indicate contentment and enjoyment. When your baby is cooing and gurgling, it's a good opportunity to engage in eye contact, play, and bonding.

Facial expressions:

Babies use facial expressions to communicate their emotions and needs. For example, a furrowed brow or pursed lips can indicate discomfort or distress, while a relaxed face and open mouth can indicate contentment and relaxation.

Body language:

Babies use body language to communicate their needs and wants. For instance, if they arch their back, flail their arms, or turn away from the breast, it could mean they are uncomfortable or want to stop breastfeeding.

Studies have shown that knowing your baby's cues and responding to them can be good for both you and your baby in many ways. For example, a study in the journal "Pediatrics" found that responsive parenting was linked to better sleep patterns, better cognitive development, and lower stress levels in both mothers and babies (Hohman et al., 2022)[1].

"By understanding your baby's cues and communication styles, you can respond effectively and build a strong bond with your baby," says pediatrician and author Dr. William Sears. "It's an important part of good parenting, and one that will pay off in countless ways in the years to come."

Understanding your baby's cues and communication styles is an important part of good parenting. By paying attention to their cries, coos, facial expressions, and body language, you can respond effectively and build a strong bond with your baby.

Coping with Sleep Deprivation and Adjusting to Parenthood

"Sleep deprivation is one of the biggest challenges of parenthood, and it can be especially difficult in the first few months," says sleep expert and author Dr. Marc Weissbluth. "But with the right techniques and support, you can get the sleep you need and adjust to parenthood successfully."

Here are some tips for coping with sleep deprivation and adjusting to parenthood:

Accept help:

---

1. Hohman, E. E. et al. (2022). Effect of the INSIGHT Firstborn Parenting Intervention on Secondborn Sleep. Pediatrics, 150(1), e2021055244. Retrieved from https://doi.org/10.1542/peds.2021-055244/

Don't be afraid to ask for help from friends, family, or a postpartum doula. Having someone to share the load can make a huge difference in your ability to cope with sleep deprivation and adjust to parenthood.

Take naps:

Napping can be a lifesaver for new parents. Whenever you have the chance, take a nap, even if it's just for a few minutes.

Get outside:

Getting outside for some fresh air and natural light can improve your mood and energy level, especially if you're feeling sleep deprived.

Seek support:

Joining a support group or seeking support from a therapist or counselor can be a great way to cope with the emotional challenges of parenthood.

"Adjusting to parenthood is a big transition, and it can be especially difficult in the first few months," says parenting expert and author Heather Armstrong. "But with the right techniques and support, you can get the sleep you need and adjust to parenthood successfully." It's important to remember that you're not alone and that help is available if you need it.

Finding Support and Community in the Early Years of Parenthood

"The early years of parenthood can be overwhelming, but it's important to remember that you're not alone," says parenting expert and author Jennifer Senior. "By finding support and community, you can get the help and encouragement you need to navigate this exciting but challenging time."

Here are some tips for finding support and community in the early years of parenthood:

- **Join a support group:**

A support group is a great way to connect with other parents who are going through the same things you are. You can share advice, offer support, and make new friends.

- **Seek online communities:**

Online communities, such as forums and social media groups, can be a great way to connect with other parents from the comfort of your own home.

- **Attend parenting classes:**

Attending parenting classes, such as childbirth education classes or infant care classes, can be a great way to connect with other parents and learn from experts.

- **Lean on friends and family:**

Don't be afraid to lean on your friends and family for support. They can offer a listening ear, a shoulder to cry on, or a helping hand when you need it.

"Finding support and community in the early years of parenthood is essential for your well-being and success as a parent," says parenting expert and author Paul Tough. "By connecting with other parents, you can get the help and encouragement you need to navigate this exciting but challenging time."

During the first few years of parenthood, it's very important to have a strong support system and a sense of community. Whether it's with a local support group, an online forum, parenting classes, or the help of friends and family, connecting with others who understand the unique challenges and joys of parenting can provide valuable resources, encouragement, and a sense of community.

Making Informed Decisions about Infant Care Practices

As a new parent, you may struggle to know what's best for your baby, especially with so many conflicting opinions around you. Decisions around your baby's sleep, feeding, and health aren't always easy to make. "Making informed decisions about infant care practices is an important part of good parenting," says pediatrician and author Dr. Harvey Karp. "By taking the time to research and understand the options, you can ensure that your baby is getting the best care possible."

Here are some tips for making informed decisions about infant care practices:

- **Research your options:**

Take the time to research your options for infant care practices, such as sleep, feeding, and vaccination. Read books, articles, and research studies, and talk to your family doctor or pediatrician.

- **Consult with experts:**

Consult with experts, such as pediatricians, lactation consultants, or sleep consultants, to get personalized advice for your baby's specific needs.

- **Consider your values:**

Consider your values and beliefs when making decisions about infant care practices. What's important to you and your family, and how does that inform your decisions about sleep, feeding, and vaccination?

- **Be open-minded:**

Be open-minded and willing to consider different perspectives and options. What works for one family might not work for another, and it's important to find what works best for you and your baby.

The following resources can help new parents learn and grow as they go through the fun and challenging process of becoming parents. Whether you're looking for information on sleep, feeding, vaccination, or any other aspect of infant care, these resources can help you make informed decisions and provide the best care possible for your baby.

Books:

"The Happiest Baby on the Block" by Dr. Harvey Karp

"The Baby Book" by Dr. William Sears and Martha Sears

"The No-Cry Sleep Solution" by Elizabeth Pantley

"The Nursing Mother's Companion" by Kathleen Huggins

"Your Baby's First Year Week by Week" by Dr. Glade Curtis and Judith Schuler

Websites:

American Academy of Pediatrics (www.aap.org)

La Leche League International (www.llli.org)

The National Sleep Foundation (www.thensf.org)

KellyMom (www.kellymom.com)

What to Expect (www.whattoexpect.com)

Making informed decisions about infant care practices is an important part of good parenting. By taking the time to research your options, consulting with experts, considering your values, and being open-minded, you can ensure that your baby is getting the best care possible.

Chapter 10

Reflecting and Embracing the Next Decade with Confidence

Reflection and Gratitude

REFLECTION AND GRATITUDE ARE powerful tools for personal growth and well-being. By taking the time to reflect on your experiences, you can gain a deeper understanding of who you are and what you value. This can lead to greater self-awareness, higher self-confidence, and a sense of purpose.

One famous quote that supports the importance of reflection is by philosopher Marcus Aurelius, who said, "The happiness of your life depends upon the quality of your thoughts." By reflecting on your thoughts and experiences, you can identify patterns and areas for growth and work toward becoming the best version of yourself.

Gratitude, on the other hand, can help you focus on the positive aspects of your life and shift your perspective from what you lack to what you have. Robert Emmons, a psychologist, has found that showing gratitude can make people feel better and lessen the symptoms of depression. As writer and motivational speaker Lou Holtz said, "It's not the load that breaks you down, it's the way you carry it." By focusing on gratitude, you can lighten your load and experience more joy and contentment in your life.

Thinking about your past and being thankful for what you have can help you learn more about yourself and view life more positively. By doing this, you can move forward with more self-awareness and confidence, ready to look forward with hope to the next ten years.

Embracing New Beginnings

Entering a new decade can bring a mix of emotions, including excitement, anxiety, and uncertainty. However, it's important to remember that new beginnings also offer the opportunity for growth and self-discovery. As author and motivational speaker Tony Robbins said, "The only way to do great work is to love what you do." By embracing new beginnings, you can explore new passions and experiences and find your true purpose and calling in life.

It's normal to feel overwhelmed and uncertain when faced with change, but it's important to remember that change is an inevitable part of life. As writer and philosopher George Bernard Shaw said, "Progress is impossible without change, and those who cannot change their minds cannot change anything." By embracing new beginnings and embracing change, you can grow and evolve into your best self.

Building Self-Confidence

Self-confidence is a crucial component of personal growth and success. It allows you to believe in yourself and your ability to tackle challenges with courage and determination. However, self-doubt can be a major obstacle to building self-confidence.

One effective technique for boosting self-confidence is positive self-talk. As motivational speaker and author Louise Hay said, "What we think about ourselves becomes the truth for us." By being kind and positive to yourself, you can fight off negative thoughts and build a more confident mindset.

Another helpful technique is to focus on your strengths and accomplishments. Writer and motivational speaker Norman Vincent Peale said, "The more you praise and celebrate your life, the more there is in life to celebrate." By focusing on your strengths and accomplishments, you can build your self-confidence and overcome self-doubt.

Embracing Challenges

Challenges are an inevitable part of life, but it's important to view them as opportunities for growth rather than obstacles to be feared. Writer and motivational speaker Mary Mann says, "A challenge only becomes an obstacle when you bow to it." You can build resilience and a growth mindset by taking on challenges and seeing them as chances to grow.

One way to become more resilient is to maintain a positive attitude and look for ways to solve problems instead of dwelling on them. As motivational speaker and author Zig Ziglar said, "You don't have to be great to start, but you have to start to be great." By focusing on solutions and taking action, you can overcome challenges and build resilience.

Another way to develop a growth mindset is to embrace learning and developing. As educator and psychologist Carol Dweck said, "The power of yet: I am not there yet, but I can get there." By having a growth mindset and putting your attention on the future, you can deal with problems effectively and reach your goals.

Setting Intentional Goals

Setting intentional goals is a crucial step toward personal and professional growth. Goals can give you direction, motivation, and a sense of purpose. As motivational speaker and author Les Brown said, "Shoot for the moon. Even if you miss, you'll land among the stars." By setting meaningful, intentional goals, you can reach for the stars and achieve your dreams.

One important tip for goal-setting is to make sure your goals are SMART: Specific, Measurable, Achievable, Relevant, and Time-bound. This helps make sure that your goals are clear, attainable, and in line with your values and priorities.

Another important step in goal-setting is to break down large goals into smaller, more manageable steps. As motivational speaker and author Brian Tracy said, "Every big accomplishment is made up of many small ones." By breaking down large goals into smaller steps, you can stay motivated and make steady progress toward your goals.

Prioritizing Self-Care

Self-care is essential for your overall well-being and should be a priority in your life. As author and motivational speaker Jim Rohn said, "Take care of your body. It's the only place you have to live." Self-care is important because it helps you protect your physical, mental, and emotional health and live a full life.

One practical tip for self-care is to make time for physical activity, such as exercise or yoga. Regular physical activity has been shown to lower stress, improve mental health, and boost self-esteem.

Another important aspect of self-care is to make time for rest and relaxation. As writer and motivational speaker Oprah Winfrey said, "You can have it all. Just not all at once." By making time for rest and relaxation, you can recharge your mental battery so that you can be more productive and focused when you return to your daily activities.

Nurturing Relationships

Relationships are very important in life. They provide support, love, and a sense of belonging. As writer and motivational speaker Deepak Chopra said, "The highest levels of happiness come from relationships." By cultivating strong relationships, you can live a happier and more fulfilling life.

One important aspect of building strong relationships is to communicate effectively and openly. As motivational speaker and author Stephen Covey said, "Seek first to understand, then to be understood." By paying attention to what other people say and saying what you think and feel in return, you can build trust and closeness in your relationships.

Another important aspect of building strong relationships is to make time for those you care about. As motivational speaker and author Jim Rohn said, "You are the average of the five people you spend the most time with." By making time for those you care about, you can build strong, meaningful relationships that bring joy and happiness to your life.

Embracing Lifelong Learning

Change is a natural and inevitable part of life, and it can be both exciting and challenging. As motivational speaker and author Tony Robbins said, "Change is inevitable. Growth is optional." By embracing change and adapting to new situations, you can grow and evolve into your best self.

To be able to accept change, it's important to have a positive attitude and focus on the possibilities that change brings. As motivational speaker and author Norman Vincent Peale said, "Change your thoughts and you change your world." By focusing on the opportunities that change brings, you can approach new situations with confidence and a sense of excitement.

Another important aspect of embracing change is being flexible and open-minded. As motivational speaker and author Brian Tracy said, "Successful people are always looking for opportunities to help others. Unsuccessful people are always asking, 'What's in it for me?'" You can adapt to new situations and find success in a world that changes quickly if you are flexible and open-minded.

Building a Legacy

Life is a journey full of ups and downs, and it's important to embrace the journey and appreciate each moment, no matter how challenging it may be. As writer and motivational speaker Dr. Seuss said, "You have brains in your head. You have feet in your shoes. You can steer yourself in any direction you choose." By embracing life's journey, you can live life to the fullest and create the experiences and memories that bring joy and meaning to your life.

One important aspect of embracing life's journey is to live in the present moment and enjoy each experience to the fullest. As motivational speaker and author Earl Nightingale said, "Never give up on a dream just because of the time it will take to accomplish it. The time will pass anyway." By living in the present moment, you can appreciate the journey you're on and find joy in each experience, no matter how challenging it may be.

Another important aspect of embracing life's journey is having a sense of purpose and direction. As motivational speaker and author Brian Tracy said, "The key to success is to focus our conscious mind on things we desire, not things we fear." You can enjoy the journey of life and find meaning and fulfillment in each experience if you have a clear sense of purpose and direction.

Looking Forward with Hope and Anticipation

Reflecting on the past decade and expressing gratitude for the experiences and people that have shaped your life is a powerful way to close one chapter and begin another. As motivational speaker and author Zig Ziglar said, "Gratitude makes sense of our past, brings peace for today, and creates a vision for tomorrow." You can appreciate your journey and look forward to a bright future if you think about the past 10 years and say thank you.

One important aspect of reflection and gratitude is to reflect on the experiences and people that have shaped your life. As motivational speaker and author John C. Maxwell said, "A grateful person is a happy person." By reflecting on the experiences and people that have shaped your life, you can express gratitude and appreciate the journey that has brought you to where you are today.

Another important aspect of reflection and gratitude is to look forward to the future with a sense of hope and excitement. As motivational speaker and author Tony Robbins said, "Life is a gift, and it offers us the privilege, opportunity, and responsibility to give something back by becoming more." By being hopeful and excited about what's next, you can enjoy the journey and look toward a bright, fulfilling future.

Conclusion

I AM GRATEFUL TO have had the opportunity to share these insights and tips with you in this book. The journey of self-discovery, purpose, and growth is one that I have been on myself, and I am inspired to help others on this journey as well.

I remember wishing that I had access to a resource like this when I was in my late 20s and 30s. At that time, I was navigating the challenges of adulting and trying to figure out who I was, what I wanted, and how to create a fulfilling life.

This book is a culmination of the lessons I have learned and the experiences I have had on my own journey. I hope that it has been helpful to you and that you have found the information and tips to be valuable.

Thank you for taking the time to read this book. If you would like more resources and support on your journey, I invite you to visit https://adultinghardbooks.com.

Here's to your continued growth, success, and happiness. Cheers to the next decade and beyond!

Also By Jeffrey C. Chapman

If you enjoyed this book, please leave a great review on Amazon. This would mean the world to me.

Also, please consider reading these other books from my series:

Adulting Hard for Young Men

Adulting Hard for Young Women

Adulting Hard After College

www.ingramcontent.com/pod-product-compliance
Ingram Content Group UK Ltd.
Pitfield, Milton Keynes, MK11 3LW, UK
UKHW022225230426
12048UKWH00016BA/1078